:: **simple** student ministry

A CLEAR PROCESS FOR STRATEGIC **YOUTH DISCIPLESHIP**

ERIC GEIGER // JEFF BORTON

B&H
PUBLISHING GROUP

NASHVILLE, TENNESSEE

ISBN: 978-0-8054-4794-1

Published by B&H Publishing Group
Nashville, Tennessee

Dewey Decimal Classification: 259.23
Subject Heading: CHURCH WORK WITH STUDENTS /
YOUTH / CHURCH GROUP WORK WITH YOUTH

4 5 6 7 8 9 10 • 22 21 20 19 18

:: **simple** student ministry

From Eric:

I dedicate this book to all the volunteers I served alongside in student ministry. I love and appreciate you and your investment in the lives of teenagers. Your labor is not in vain.
(1 Cor. 15:58)

From Jeff:

I dedicate this book to my wife, Jennifer. Your strength and creativity amazes me. Your love completes me. "The LORD has done great things for us, and we are filled with joy" (Ps. 126:3 NIV).

Contents

Acknowledgments

I love the staff I currently serve with because many of us are current or former student pastors. And so much of student ministry is still in our blood: the expectation that God could radically change someone, the relational focus, the understanding that relevant communication is not an option, and the desire to lead a movement and not just an organization. Thanks to the team at Christ Fellowship.

I am also eternally grateful for the adult volunteers with whom I was honored to partner with during my years as a student pastor. I think of you and praise God because of your partnership in the gospel (Phil. 1:3–5). Names such as Sims, McKillen, Overmyer, Burkhart, Bowman, Barnard, and many others from my student ministry days in Cincinnati still elicit an overwhelming sense of gratitude.

I thank Jeff, not only for his work on this project but also for his phenomenal leadership in student ministry. I have told people that Jeff is a more effective student pastor than I ever was. And I mean it.

Most of all I thank my wife, Kaye, who always served alongside me during our days in student ministry. From counseling girls to hosting students in our home to leading small groups, her investment in teenagers has made an eternal difference. And serving alongside her caused me to love her more.

I thank you who are reading because of your love for students. Your labor is not in vain. Thank you for pouring yourself into students. I pray you may do so even more effectively after reading this book.

—Eric Geiger

■　■　■

I am thankful for the volunteers I have served with in my years of student ministry. Thank you for serving students because of your love for Jesus. Student ministry would be impossible without you.

The Christ Fellowship staff is one of the most talented and creative groups of people I have ever met. I'm thankful to be part of a team that takes sharing Jesus seriously, but the team members don't take themselves seriously. Reaching Miami for Jesus with you is a blast.

I'm thankful for Pastor and Mrs. Bowen who invested five years in my life. I benefited greatly from your shepherding, love, and direction.

I thank Tony Isaacs for my youth internship in college. You have taught me the value of relationships, and I learned so much from watching your life.

I thank Jorge and Tim; your influences continually point me to God. You truly sharpen me.

My family has been a constant source of comfort and encouragement. I'm thankful for your love and support. Mom, Jodi, Sue, and the rest of the family, I love you.

I'm thankful for Eric. Your leadership and dedication to advance the kingdom is unmatched. I am humbled to serve with you and grateful for the opportunities you have given me.

My beautiful wife, Jen: You sacrifice more than anyone so that I can do ministry. Your patience, understanding, and work ethic only make me love you more. I love living my life with you. Thank you for loving and leading girls in student ministry.

To the reader: Thank you for loving teenagers. Our prayer is that this book will be a great resource to you as you disciple students. Be strong in the Lord.

—Jeff Borton

CHAPTER ONE

Student Ministry Breakfast Sandwiches

Why did you have to go
and make things so complicated?

—Pop singer, Avril Lavigne

Starbucks shut down.

Don't worry. Everything is fine now. The closing was temporary. You can still get your coffee fix and stand in line and display your cultural savvy by ordering a triple-shot drink that baffles the customer behind you.

Howard Schultz, the leader of the company, made the newsworthy decision to temporarily close all Starbucks in the United States.

He observed that the baristas were losing their edge in brewing the perfect cup of coffee. In the formative years of Starbucks, the attention of the baristas was on the coffee.

But with the emergence of other food items and music, their attention became divided. And the quality of the coffee and the customer experience spiraled downward.

So Schultz called a time-out. Starbucks needed to return to the essence of Starbucks, to its core mission.

On Tuesday, February 26, 2008, approximately seven thousand Starbucks were closed for three hours. And during those three hours, approximately one hundred thirty-five thousand employees were retrained in making coffee.

Schultz also made the decision that Starbucks would reduce the variety of breakfast sandwiches made and sold. Why would he make such a move?

The smell of the sandwiches was competing with the aroma of coffee. And the aroma of coffee is essential in the Starbucks experience.

Closing seven thousand stores for several hours was a costly decision. But the decision refocused the company on its essence—great coffee. Offering fewer breakfast sandwiches must not have been a popular decision with everyone, but the move revealed a renewed commitment to the essence of Starbucks.

We need a renewed commitment to the essence of the gospel, to the essence of the movement of the church. And we need a renewed commitment to the essence of student ministry.

Our lives and the lives of the people we lead are to be the aroma of Christ.

For we are to God the aroma of Christ among those who are being saved and those who are perishing. To the one we are the smell of death; to the other, the fragrance of life. (2 Cor. 2:15–16 NIV)

The aroma of Christ should stand out in our lives.

And in our student ministries.

But often the smell of the breakfast sandwiches gets in the way. The smell of the numerous programs cluttering our student ministries overwhelms the aroma of Christ. Busy calendars, lost focus, overprogrammed weeks, and directionless ministries have steered us away from our core mission.

Yet Another Event

It's a Saturday morning . . . about 4 a.m.

The aroma of seventh-grade boys, who insist deodorant is overrated, fills the church fellowship hall. The students are so wired on Red Bull and M&M's that even the easygoing students have morphed into some strange anomaly of caffeine, adrenaline, and hormones.

The parents roped into being chaperones for a dangerously acceptable "leader:student ratio" are in awe while faithfully attempting to execute their responsibilities. One leader is strategically placed to ensure kids do not "make out" in the sanctuary. Another leader sits near the food tables, eyes glossed over, trying to convince himself and everyone else that he's still "got it" in terms of hanging out with students. Everyone knows he's really out like a beat-up prizefighter.

The leaders are wondering what they were thinking when they planned this beast, the annual all-nighter. Perhaps the Enemy concocted the idea.

Sensing the discouragement, the student pastor is sheepishly trying to convince some of his leaders that the night is *so worth it.*

He holds up a stack of guest cards and talks about the great relationships being formed. To further build his case, he counts the number of volunteers and multiplies the number by twelve—the hours of the all-nighter. *Wow. We have poured hundreds of hours into teenagers in one night!*

A few of the students thank him for the night. They had a great time and the all-nighter is so much better than staying at home with a normal bedtime. When he asks about their older siblings' absence, he discovers that he is no longer needed to plan their social lives.

Thirty minutes before the much-anticipated ending of the all-nighter, the student pastor attempts to motivate students to help clean up. All he gets is blank stares. Evidently the 2 a.m. Bible study on serving did not stick.

Alone, he hauls trash to the Dumpster and reflects on the night. His thoughts go far beyond whether the students are having a good time or not. He begins to consider some ramifications that lead him past the 7 a.m. pickup time.

How will this all-nighter benefit our student ministry?
Or the students?

While he attempted to rally the troops with the number of guest cards, he failed to mention that most of the guests were students from other churches.

While he bragged on the number of volunteer hours invested in the students, truthfully he wishes he could utilize those hours at other times. He is perpetually short on volunteers for Bible study groups.

He has been rehearsing the pitch he will make to the potential leaders who chaperoned the event. *But will they still want to be a part of student ministry after tonight?*

And he knows the students need more than mere chaperones who stand on the side and give a watchful eye to the sophomore guy who is grateful for the attention from the middle school girls. He wants the students to receive nurture and care from God-fearing adults who invest time and energy into students.

Yet tonight was the antithesis of a group of adults shepherding teenagers. Tonight was mere herding, gently described as chaperoning.

He stands by the Dumpster, frustrated.

His wife is home with his four-year-old. He has not finished his message for the students on Sunday. He wants to sleep but knows he must finish his talk sometime today. And most of all, he wants to spend some time with his family. The next thirty-six hours are going to be insane.

He hopes that the amount of time the event took away from his preparation for the Sunday morning program will pay off in some way. All the details of food, games, permission forms, securing volunteers, and phone calls have consumed him for the last two days.

Hopefully, one of the few unchurched guests will desire to come back to the student ministry service on Wednesday night. Of course, the service won't be anything like the all-nighter.

He reflects on his event-planning skills. Most of the thanks related to the night are about the crazy games or extra "free time."

Is this really what God called me to do? Plan the social lives of these kids?

He pulls out his cell phone and glances at a photo of his kid. He wants to be home. And he feels guilty for wanting to be home.

Maybe you have felt the same way. Perhaps you feel the frustration of the realization that your student ministry is full of the breakfast sandwiches that distract from the essence of your ministry.

Perhaps you've been frustrated by the lack of discipleship in the midst of the abundance of activity. The calendar is full, but you don't feel full. There is a pang of wondering that student ministry should be different.

Must be different.

How did student ministry become so complicated and busy?

Expectations

One of the reasons student ministries become complicated is the expectation of others. Many church members expect student ministry to be busy. Perhaps when you were recruited into student ministry, you heard the advice, "Keep the kids busy to keep them out of trouble."

So, how do you plan to keep your students busy? If you don't give them plenty of options, they'll succumb to the wiles of the devil!

Holiness is much deeper than keeping kids out of trouble. It takes much more than a busy church calendar to influence students to live holy and pure lives. If a student's purity depends on a program, what happens during the other hours in the week?

And holiness includes "our kids" transforming the lives of others, not being removed from the culture.

Your calling is deeper than running programs to keep kids busy. The version of Matthew 28:19 in your Bible does not read, "Go and keep Christian teenagers busy." If it does, you need a new translation.

Deep down you were never really burdened to program a Fifth Quarter, SNAC (Sunday night after church), Death by Pizza, Afterglow, or some other lame event with a dumb name.

Likewise, some parents expect the student ministry to be busy. Not only is the expectation to plan an elaborate trip for the students, but fund-raisers to finance the trip must be planned as well.

Eric recalls the time early in his student ministry days when he was hospitalized with a stomach virus acquired during a pancake supper fund-raiser, which brought in a whopping two hundred bucks.

Jeff will never forget the moment the mother of one of his students approached him about creating more programming. The student ministry was taking a trip to Mississippi to help rebuild homes for a week after Hurricane Katrina. The cost of the trip was $130 per student.

When the mother was notified the student ministry didn't have any more scholarships available for the trip, she informed Jeff that the student ministry should provide fund-raisers to help pay for the trip.

The expectation was that the student ministry was not only responsible for hosting a mission trip, but also ensuring everyone was able to pay for it without any level of personal sacrifice.

Think about it. Fund-raisers are events to finance other events. No, thank you. And we know washing cars with students is a great bonding moment, but do we have to ask people in the community for money? What if we simply served them?

Not only do some church members and parents secretly crave that student ministries will be complex with an abundance of programming, some teenagers hold the same expectation.

Where are we going for camp this year?

I hope the retreat is better than last year's . . . even though the blob was awesome!

Remember the fat kid who sent the skinny kid into outer space? Yeah! That rocked!

The memories. Without these great memories it would be hard to forget the countless hours of planning, recruiting, and praying for the trip. The budget for that camp alone could have floated a third world country for a weekend, but at least we have the T-shirts.

Eric failed to meet the expectations of some students because he did not offer an all-nighter his last six years in student ministry (including the all-nighter without food, which should not be called a fast because no one was praying). When kids would ask, "When are we having a lock-in?" Eric's standard response became, "When are you going to have a quiet time?" Most kids asking for a lock-in are "carnal churched freshmen" who do not have their driver's license and want the student ministry to plan their social lives.

Most of our student ministries are known for camps, retreats, programs, choir tours, ski-trips, fund-raisers, and all-nighters. And few are known for the sweet aroma of Christ in the lives of teenagers.

There are pressure and expectations from outside the church as well, pressure from others in student ministry.

Come to this conference! Your student ministry will be changed forever! Your students will love God, transform their schools, and thank you for it! All you have to do is show up!

Other student ministry leaders talk about the great band, awesome speaker, and number of busloads they took to camp. It's like a merit badge to throw a monster camp and take more students than there were wandering Israelites.

Still other leaders talk about their busy student ministry. They (seemingly) have the resources and volunteers to offer something almost every night of the week. And you should too!

Traditions

Expectations aren't the only factor in complex student ministry programming; there are also programs, events, and traditions that have been handed down. Perhaps you inherited a slate of programs, and your worth is evaluated by how you manage what you inherited.

We aren't suggesting that all traditions are bad.

Traditions can be really fun. At Christmas, some families cut down a tree together or pull the one from Target out of the closet and "install" it. Some enjoy decorating their tree and putting up lights as a way to spend time together. Other families actually make popcorn and construct popcorn garlands. Both delicious and functional. Some traditions are great and should be observed, but other traditions are simply a waste of time, energy, and resources.

Student ministries can live out traditions that are irrelevant to the formation of students' spiritual lives. In conversations with student ministries across the country, we discovered that many still run at least one program that seems pointless. When asked, *Why do you offer this?* the typical answer is, *We just always have.* There is no measure to the program's overall effectiveness in light of an overarching process of discipleship.

Routine keeps the program on the calendar.

Amos, prophet and servant of God, understood what it meant to be surrounded by people who worshipped God in a routine manner, who gathered without a desire to encounter Him.

Israel enjoyed a time of prosperity, but in this prosperity the people lost sincerity in their worship of God. No longer were the sacrifices and the worship centered on Jehovah but rather on the routine. The disobedient, covenant-breaking Israel was simply honoring God out of tradition and not out of a sincere heart. And God was disgusted.

> "I hate, I despise your religious feasts; I cannot stand
> your assemblies. Even though you bring me burnt
> offerings and grain offerings, I will not accept them.
> Though you bring choice fellowship offerings, I will
> have no regard for them." (Amos 5:21–22 NIV)

If we choose to settle for the routine instead of a passionate desire to see Christ formed in the students we lead, we are behaving like Israel in Amos's day. If we toss up a religious feast of a program because the program has always been done, sincerity and passion are missing. And we are inviting God to our own religious feast.

Maintaining programs. Planning events. Begging students to attend a conference because someone overestimated how many students would attend and the deposit is nonrefundable and nontransferable. Is this what God intends for student ministry? Is this what you are called to do?

Deficient Discipleship

We can attempt to pass the blame of our complicated student ministries to the expectations of others or the cluttered programming we inherited. But we must also own the problem.

Often, our view of discipleship is deficient.

Many ministries possess a faulty definition of discipleship, which in turn leads to faulty discipleship. Many leaders equate discipleship with knowledge, but discipleship is much broader than knowledge. Jesus commanded us to "go and make disciples . . . teaching them to *obey* everything I have commanded" (Matt. 28:19–20 NIV, emphasis added). The end result of discipleship is not merely the knowledge of all Jesus commanded but the *obedience* of all Jesus commanded.

True discipleship is not about information but transformation.

Obedience, not knowledge, is the bottom line of discipleship. Many ministries claim to be big on discipleship; however, the disciples being produced seldom look like the disciples Jesus produced.

Discipleship is not a program. The solution to the increasing discipleship problem in our student ministries is not another program. Or another shot of curriculum.

Discipleship is a process.

Spiritual maturation and true transformation are a process that God brings us through as we encounter Him daily.

> Now the Lord is the Spirit, and where the Spirit of the Lord is, there is freedom. And we, who with unveiled faces all reflect the Lord's glory, are being transformed into his likeness with ever-increasing glory, which comes from the Lord, who is the Spirit. (2 Cor. 3:17–18 NIV)

In the crucial passage above, the apostle Paul was teaching about spiritual transformation, using the life of Moses as an illustration. Moses would walk up Mount Sinai and meet with God face-to-face. Each time Moses would meet with God, he would come down from the mountain glowing. The encounter with God was so remarkable that Moses was transformed each time. His appearance was altered. He shone. He looked different.

Any encounter with God transforms us.

But once Moses left the presence of God, the glory would fade. As he walked down the mountain, his radiance would decrease. So he wore a veil to cover the fading glory.

Yet Paul was saying we have *unveiled* faces. We do not need a cover-up. We do not wear a veil because the glory of God is not diminishing in our lives. In fact, the opposite is true. The glory is ever increasing. We never leave the presence of God. We never come down the mountain because God's presence is in us. His Spirit lives within us. We enjoy a relationship with God that even Moses did not.

So we are *being transformed*.

The word for *transform* is in the passive voice and present tense. The passive voice indicates that we do not transform ourselves nor do the students we lead transform themselves. God is the one who does the transforming. The present tense indicates that this transforming is happening now. We were not only transformed in the past, but God is doing a work in us right now.

The word from transformation is *metamorphosis*. The powerful word means to change the essential nature of something. Metamorphosis speaks of real change, not just a change on the outside. The core of something is changed. The word is used to describe the process a caterpillar goes through to become a butterfly. The nasty, wormy, creepy crawly insect becomes a beautiful butterfly.

Several years ago a popular television show for children was the *Mighty Morphin Power Rangers*. The characters in the show were normal teenagers, but they also had the ability to morph into Power Rangers with special powers. They would be transformed into supernatural heroes. In moments of crisis, they would say, "It's morphing time."

It is morphing time.

God desires to morph you. And He desires to morph the students God has called you to lead. He is seeking to transform them into His image. And He wants to do so with ever-increasing glory.

Metamorphosis/transformation is a process. Thus we must help those we lead engage Christ in the process of spiritual transformation.

But without a clear understanding of discipleship as a process, student ministry leaders have the tendency to offer programs and events with no understanding of how all they offer fits into a comprehensive plan or process for discipleship. Without an understanding of process, programs are offered as Band-Aids for a myriad of problems in the lives of teenagers instead of strategic steps to help nudge students along on the process of life transformation.

Despite the reality that discipleship is a process, an understanding of process is woefully lacking in church leaders. Thus our ministries become complicated and directionless as more and more programs are offered to meet a real or perceived need without regard for the whole picture.

A simple and strategic process for discipleship of students will be the lens from which expectations and traditions are viewed.

Howard Schultz of Starbucks made a bold move.

As a leader, would you be willing to make a bold move?

Like Schultz of Starbucks, would you call a time-out? Would you be willing to evaluate what might be getting in the way of helping students live as the aroma of Christ in their schools and communities?

The stakes were high for Starbucks. But the stakes are even higher for you. Your role is more significant. You are investing your life, not in overpriced lattes but in students who God desires to mobilize to transform and impact this world.

CHAPTER TWO

Simple Student Ministry?

Simplicity is the ultimate sophistication.

—Leonardo da Vinci

I s there really such a thing as simple student ministry?

We are encouraging your ministry to students to be simple. We know students are not simple. They are extremely complex. Physically, socially, and cognitively they are internally experiencing an immense amount of change in the midst of an externally confusing world.

They are trapped between childhood and adulthood. They are adults trying to happen; consequently, they are the most complex demographic we minister to. And their complexity only heightens the need for the ministry designed for them to be simple and strategic.

To effectively disciple students in the context of a student ministry, a simple process must be designed and executed.

Amazingly, people read the book *Simple Church* and walked away with a new "model" for ministry. *Simple Church* was never intended to be a model. In fact, the first sentence in the book reads, "Relax. This is not about another church model."[1]

Topics that would need to be discussed in a book propagating a church model are not discussed in *Simple Church*. Issues such as music style, version of the Bible to use in teaching, or church architecture aren't mentioned. Leadership structure is not even addressed. For example, the book does not encourage churches to be pastor led, staff led, elder led, or even unbiblically deacon led. Church polity is not discussed because a model is not being pushed.

The truth is that *Simple Church* was the result of a nerdy research project. The major discovery that led to the writing of the book is that there is a highly significant relationship between vibrant and growing churches and churches with a simple process for discipleship.

The key concept in *Simple Church* is not in the word *simple*. The key concept is in the word *process*.

All churches and all ministries should have a *process* for making disciples regardless of the format, style, location, or demographic. Since discipleship is the biblical mandate, a *process* for making disciples must be present in all ministries.

The fact that people looked for a new model for ministry in *Simple Church* is alarming and disturbing. And it points to our proclivity as leaders to search for models or programs instead of wrestling with a *process* for making disciples in the context of our ministry environments.

Simple Student Ministry will apply the concepts of *Simple Church* in the context of student ministry. While new statistical (quantitative) research has not been conducted, qualitative research has been conducted via case studies of churches and parachurch ministries that exemplify effectively moving students through a process of discipleship. You will likely read about a ministry similar to yours and learn how it has implemented a simple process.

Simple Student Ministry will encourage you to design a process for discipleship in your student ministry. The process should be crystal clear (clarity) and move students to greater levels of spiritual commitment (movement). All of your programs and leaders should be aligned (alignment) to the process God gives you. And you should leverage (focus) all your energy and resources on your discipleship process.

While many student ministries are personality program, or event driven, *Simple Student Ministry* emphasizes your discipleship process as the driving factor behind your programming.

Again, this is not a model. One style does not fit all. There is not a cookie-cutter way to do student ministry. This book will challenge you to design a process for your ministry regardless if it is big, small, downtown, or next to a national forest in the middle of nowhere.

Why Simple Student Ministry?

While all ministries and churches should have a simple and strategic process for making disciples, a process-centered approach to ministry is especially crucial in student ministry. A student ministry with a simple process creates space for relationships, engages students in ministry and mission, fosters less dependence on programs, and operates with great intentionality.

Creates Space for Relationships

Teenagers need relationships with godly adults. Teenagers see little consistency in this world, and they need to be confronted with the consistency of Christ through an adult who loves Jesus and them.

A simple process in student ministry reduces the number of programs that volunteer leaders need to attend. Thus the decluttered calendar provides more opportunities for adult leaders to relationally invest in students outside of the ministry programming. Less programming creates space for vital relationships to occur between adults and students.

And discipling others has always been relational.

The apostle Paul instructed the Christians at Philippi, "Do what you have learned and received and heard and seen in me" (Phil. 4:9). His appeal was very relational. *Do what you saw me do.*

Discipleship is not merely information transfer; it is life transfer. Too many of our student ministries recruit "teachers" to pour information into students instead of recruiting and training leaders to invest their lives in teenagers.

Teaching is a vital part of discipleship but it is only *one* part. Discipleship occurs when a leader models and teaches the whole life of Christ to a student and the student begins to imitate that life (1 Cor. 11:1).

Jesus did not approach His discipleship group with a paperback book. He approached them with His life. He taught through His life. He said, "I am the bread of life" (John 6:35), and then fed five thousand men. He said, "I am the light of the world" (John 9:5), and then put light into a blind man's eyes. He said, "I am the resurrection and the life" (John 11:25), and then raised a dead man.

His life discipled the Twelve.

Jesus is God and He could have chosen any method to bring people to Himself, to ensure the gospel would carry on after He departed, and to ensure we would experience the joy of knowing Him. He could have chosen any strategy, and He chose to relationally pour Himself into a group of individuals.

Since discipleship as a whole is relational, discipleship with students is even more so because of the nature of teenagers. Students are already relational. Developmentally, adolescents find their identity through their relationships.

They adopt the moral values of those closest to them, and their faith is very interdependent with those they trust and respect.

This is exciting news if our student ministries are filled with godly adults ready to reproduce themselves in students. This is alarming news if we don't have adults willing to invest in students.

If we do not invest in students, someone else will.

Jesus poured Himself into His disciples. He took them everywhere and exposed them to His life, mission, and ministry. A quick scan through the gospel of Mark shows how Jesus lived among and built meaningful relationships with His disciples:

- He took them on road trips. (1:21)
- He went to their homes. (1:29)
- He met their families. (1:31)
- He took them to dinner parties. (2:15)
- He cruised the countryside with them. (2:23)
- He broke rules with them. (2:24; 3:1–2)
- He withdrew from everyone else to be with them. (3:7; 4:35)
- He took them to other people's homes. (3:20)
- He ate with them. (3:20)
- He went boating with them. (4:36)
- He relaxed and slept in front of them. (4:38)
- He got kicked out of places with them. (5:17)
- He brought them home with Him. (6:1)

- He took them to church. (6:2)
- He rested with them. (6:31)
- He desired to listen to them and know them. (6:30–32)
- He took them mountain climbing. (9:2)
- He stayed up late with them. (11:11)
- He looked at sights with them. (13:1)
- He celebrated holidays with them. (14:12)
- He took them to His favorite places. (14:32)
- He shared personal struggles with them. (14:34)

A cluttered student ministry calendar utilizes volunteer leaders to run programs for students. A simple student ministry frees up godly adults to initiate relationships with students at key programs *and* significantly invest in students outside of the programs. In short, complex student ministry offers ministry *for* students while simple student ministry creates space for leaders to build discipleship relationships *with* students.

Engages Students in Ministry and Mission

Students are extremely altruistic. They want their lives to matter. They are attracted to causes. At the same time, students learn best by doing. They learn the most when they are debriefing in the midst of action.

Sadly, local community groups and school clubs offer more engaging causes for students to join than many student ministries. The church has the greatest cause in the history of the world—displaying the gospel to the world around us. But we often lock students in program after program instead of unleashing them to serve the world around them. And by doing so, we limit their learning and growth.

A student ministry with a simple process engages students in ministry and mission because ministry and mission are a part of the discipleship process. The process includes moving students to significant ministry and life mission instead of shelling students up in a complex set of weekly programs.

Fosters Less Dependence on Programs

A student ministry with a strategic process intentionally moves students to a place where they own their faith. Instead of merely attending programs, students become leaders and learn how to develop themselves spiritually.

The next big thing on the calendar mind-set is an assassin to a student's spiritual life. When students believe that God engages them only at big events, they subconsciously accept that God speaks to them only in *those* places. Thus, students who have a steady diet of these events get programmed to look for God only there. They don't see their daily lives as opportunities to walk with God. Instead of learning to train themselves to be godly (see 1 Tim. 4:7), they are trained to anticipate a big event when God will meet with them.

Similarly to a spiritual drug addiction, they are craving their next connection to God via a big event with a funnier speaker, a better band, louder music, and more pizza.

Student ministry leaders often wish these events could last forever because of what happens when the event is over. But the "camp high" is short-lived. In spite of the morning devotional on the beach about how *not to let the fire die*, it does. And the return to normal life is painful to watch.

Sadly, the overprogrammed approach to student ministry continues to fail. Ed Stetzer, director of LifeWay Research, made a profound observation about what really connects students to their faith for a lifetime. Stetzer noted:

> Teens are looking for more from a youth ministry
> than a holding tank with pizza. They look for a
> church that teaches them how to live life. As they
> enter young adulthood, church involvement that has
> made a difference in their lives gives them a powerful
> reason to keep attending.[2]

We must recognize that a student's commitment to an event or a pizza party is not a commitment to grow in their faith. Busyness does not lead to godliness.

Complicated student ministries foster an unhealthy dependence on big events and ministry programming. Students jump from event to event without learning how to develop themselves spiritually. Student ministries with a simple and strategic process have less of a tendency to foster the unhealthy relationship with programs because less programming is offered. And more attention is given to helping the student walk with God outside of a program.

Pastors have often said about our personal lives, "If Satan cannot get you to sin, he will just get you busy." If that statement is true in our personal lives, is the same statement not true in our ministries? If busyness hurts our personal lives, does it not have the same effect on our ministries?

The busyness offered by a cluttered and complicated student ministry may actually be doing more harm than good.

Operates with Great Intentionality

Our God is intentional.

Creation showcases God's intentionality. God very purposely and systematically created the universe *ex nihilo* (something out of nothing). He placed the stars, world, and sun in synchronized orbit. Thousands of exact measurements and processes keep our universe in a functional condition that sustains life.

He also displayed his intentionally in our redemption. He entered our world "at just the right time" (Rom. 5:6 NIV) to offer Himself as the one and only perfect sacrifice for our sins (see Rom. 5:17).

We must reflect God's intentionality in our design of a student ministry strategy.

All ministries should be conducted intentionally, not haphazardly. But intentionality is especially crucial in student ministry because of the brevity of the opportunity. We have a short amount of time to impact students.

And the stakes are high.

The majority of people who become followers of Christ do so before they graduate high school. We must be evangelistically intentional in our approach to student ministry.

Additionally, many significant life decisions are made within years of high school graduation. The character developed in students during their adolescent years will quickly be manifested in their life choices as they move into adulthood. Young adults will likely choose an educational plan, a career path, and a spouse; therefore, we must equip them intentionally to make wise choices.

Furthermore, students are the influencers in our culture. They form and build the culture we live in. As leaders of students, you have the privilege of investing in the most pursued demographic of people in the world. While major marketing companies look to students for purchasing trends and bigger sales, God sees students as His ambassadors in a dark world. As a leader of students, God has placed you in a position to help produce transformation in a group of people He desires to use to transform others, our culture, and our world. Their potential to revolutionize our world demands intentionality in ministry.

The hogfish is a fish that lives in the warm waters of the Atlantic Ocean off the coast of Florida and throughout the Caribbean. Many fishermen and seafood connoisseurs alike would argue that the hogfish could quite possibly be one of the best-tasting fish, even more so than a grouper or a dorado (the perpetual "catch of the day" known as mahi-mahi).

Hogfish have many interesting characteristics. They are easily identified by their long, beak-like mouth and tough to catch with a rod and reel. They also possess the ability to camouflage themselves almost instantaneously to blend in with their immediate environment.

To catch a hogfish, you must be both intentional and incarnational.

If a fisherman were standing in a boat, still tied to the dock, firing spear after spear into the water in hopes of shooting a hogfish, he should be quickly advised that his efforts are in vain. He has a much better chance of hurting himself than he does killing a hogfish.

The fisherman must jump into the water with a mask, snorkel, fins, and a speargun. He must enter the world of a hogfish.

The fisherman who remains on the dock, firing spears is not being intentional. He is merely hoping for the best with no real plan. He has the right tools, but with no plan for execution, he'll go home empty-handed.

Or maybe he has just never heard there's a better way to fish.

Perhaps you need to understand that there is a better way, a more intentional way, to do student ministry. Student ministry leaders must be both incarnational and intentional.

We must incarnationally step into the lives of our students as Jesus stepped into our lives. And we must approach our ministries with an intentional strategy, knowing how we are going to lead students spiritually through their formative years. We must be careful not to merely fire program after program at students, hoping one will make an impact.

Many leaders in student ministry would admit that their current ministry is not what they initially sensed God calling them to do. All the programs, fund-raisers, events, and trips that everyone believes is part of student ministry blur the original calling. They sensed God nudging them to disciple students. Now they manage programs and plan trips with little intentionality.

Have you ever thought, *God, thank You for calling me into the planning ministry! Thank You for letting me be a travel agent. Thank You for letting my schedule be so packed that discipleship is only a small part of our bigger picture. Thank You for all the nights away from my family so I can continue to be frustrated!*

No. Nope. No way.

Now What?

Perhaps you realize that your student ministry lacks an overarching process for discipleship. Perhaps you realize with all the programming, your student ministry lacks intentionality and the opportunity for leaders to live incarnationally with students.

In the next several chapters, we will discuss the four key elements to a simple process in student ministry: clarity, movement, alignment, and focus. These elements are based on the original research in *Simple Church* and have been confirmed in case studies of effective student ministries. At the end of each core chapter, we are placing discussion questions to wrestle with as a student ministry leadership team.

Let's begin . . .

CHAPTER THREE

Clarity

I can see clearly now the rain is gone.

—Johnny Nash

Stand-up comedian/actor Jeff Foxworthy has popularized the phrase, "You might be a redneck if . . ." Many of Foxworthy's entertaining redneck qualifications are accurate, maybe even sting a little to our student ministry friends in the south. (Miami is not the south. Miami is North Cuba.)

The sting is the realization that something said touched a tender nerve and leaves you thinking, *Wait, I do that!* Hopefully these don't strike a chord with you:

- You might be a redneck if you and your dog are on the same medication.
- You might be a redneck if you and your wife have the same haircut.[1]

Identifying if you are a redneck is pretty easy. And painfully funny.

Identifying if your ministry is complex might be as easy. If discipleship isn't clearly defined, your ministry is complex. If clarity is lacking, a multitude of ideas has your ministry running in a myriad of directions. Here are some easy ways to identify if you are complex:

- You might be complex if you inherited a program called SNAC (Sunday night after church) and have no idea why you offer it.

- You might be complex if your students think small group means the number of people who fit into a Hyundai Accent when playing yet another game involving a red light on the way to yet another retreat.

- You might be complex if you can wear a different student ministry T-shirt every day for two weeks.

- You might be complex if a student has to choose between summer camp, choir tour, vacation Bible school leadership, and a potluck supper in the same month.

- You might be even more complex if you actually believe a student should do all of the above in the same month.

- You might be complex if you can't lead a mission trip over spring break because of a scheduled revival week, complete with homecoming dinner.

- You might be complex if the only ministry opportunity your students are offered is caring for the live animals during the annual Christmas program. Or passing out the offering plates on Young People Sunday.
- You might be complex if your leaders confuse a pizza party with discipleship.
- You might be complex if you have to gain approval from more than one committee to purchase an Xbox.

While some of the complex qualifiers are entertaining, they are painful for those who can relate. Admitting that ministry programming and an unclear ministry philosophy clutter a clear path for discipleship is painful. Without a clearly defined process (a ministry blueprint from which to build), student ministries are subject to a myriad of complexities.

The Need for a Blueprint

Grand Central Station is a fascinating place to visit. Walking the station feels like touring history. At almost one hundred years old, the architecture is ornate and impressive. The giant clock and the hustle and bustle of New York City glamorize the aging terminal.

Movies with a love story have romanticized the station. Couples meet there and fall in love. Others take the last train out of the city. Some people miss the train, and their opportunities fade away as the train fades into the distance.

Grand Central Station is also extremely effective, as it hosts thousands of travelers per day. It is a hub of transportation that houses massive train tracks on two levels. In 1903 the architectural firm of Reed and Stem won the right to design the blueprints for the historic station. On February 2, 1913, it opened for business. Since that day, millions of people have traveled through the station.[2]

Copious planning, substantial financing, a building contractor, and most important, the right set of blueprints were necessary for building.

Blueprints are the one-dimensional design that results in a three-dimensional reality. The blueprints for Grand Central Station dictated *how* the station was to be built. Given the size of the station, the blueprints must have been enormous.

Building projects of all sizes and scope utilize a contractor. Contractors can visualize the completed project, and they know what steps are required to effectively design and build. The contractor lives by the blueprint.

If you intend to build a replica of Grand Central Station, a digital picture and strong back will not suffice. You will need the original blueprint and a much bigger backyard.

As the blueprint brought direction and cohesion to the building of Grand Central Station, a ministry blueprint is essential in designing and building an effective student ministry. Without a blueprint that brings clarity, student ministry leaders will attempt to build without direction or an overarching plan.

Student Ministry Blueprint

The blueprint for building a student ministry is a discipleship process.

A process gives direction and clarity as to *how* students' lives will be built and constructed. A process describes *how* discipleship will be carried out in the context of a student ministry.

A clear ministry blueprint guides us to spiritually build the lives of students. As a leader of students, your work is similar to that of a contractor. Your calling is to partner with God to build students.

> It was he who gave some to be apostles, some to be prophets, some to be evangelists, and some to be pastors and teachers, to prepare God's people for works of service, so that the body of Christ may be built up. (Eph. 4:11–12 NIV)

Because we take the call of God to minister to students very seriously, our *how* in making student disciples must also be taken seriously. Any structure of significance should not be built without a blueprint. And neither should the body of Christ.

By the grace God has given me, I laid a foundation as
an expert builder, and someone else is building on it.
But each one should be careful *how* he builds.
(1 Cor. 3:10 NIV, emphasis added)

Expert builders come to the table with more than a
picture of what will be built. Expert builders come with
a clear blueprint, a clear process, a clear *how*. And as a
student ministry leader, you must be an expert builder. You
must come to the table with more than a killer work ethic
and a digital picture of what you desire to build.

Simple student ministries design a clear discipleship
process. Strategically created programs are placed along
the points of the stated process to help move students
through the designed process in order to build their walk
with God.

Complex student ministries offer their programs without regard to an overarching blueprint. What is popular
in the culture of student ministry often defines discipleship for complex ministries. When the student ministry
barometer changes, the programming changes. The means
to consistent discipleship is unclear. The "next big thing" is
never consistent.

With no clear blueprint, everyone has an opinion of
what student ministry should look like in a specific context.
In the example of a building project, multiple contractors
with no blueprint working on the same house would be a
nightmare. Different approaches converging on the same
project would be chaos. In the same way, an amalgam of

ideas and programs cannot be implemented in hopes of building an effective student ministry.

How are you building?

Student ministries build up the body of Christ by discipling students to impact the world. And *how* discipleship is designed and executed will define the type of student we produce.

The *How*

In our observations of student ministries, we discovered that most student ministries have not determined *what* type of student they seek to build. These ministries simply exist, offering programs and events with no sense of direction and no understanding of how the programs contribute to the overall picture. In these ministries, the leaders have not even agreed on *what* they are building.

Much less *how* they are building.

Ministries without a clear *what* are led by leaders who approach the weekly student ministry programs with no goal. Programs are led without any forethought or sense of mission. These ministries tend to bounce from idea to idea in an endless quest for something (anything) that will work.

However, some student ministries do know *what* they want to accomplish in the lives of students, *what* type of student disciple they would like to build. And these student ministries should be commended for thinking strategically about their ministries, for initiating discussions on what their ultimate goal or end game is. Programs are planned to help realize the stated goal. Leaders are rallied around the purpose of the ministry.

Typically in ministries with a clear *what*, a vision statement, a purpose statement, or even an ethos describes the type of student the ministry aims to produce. Here is a typical student ministry statement:

> The purpose of the student ministries at "Yada Yada Church" is to help students gain a personal faith in Christ that will enable them to make godly decisions as adults who make an impact on the world.

The desired outcome for a student is articulated. The statement looks great on a letterhead or a parent newsletter. And we would applaud the leaders for desiring students to make wise choices and impact their world.

However, a clear process is lacking. The blueprint is missing. The *what* has been defined, but the *how* is unclear. An unclear *how* is commonplace in student ministry.

A student ministry should be clear about its purpose for existence. Anyone who is in ministry to "keep students busy and out of trouble" should leave the ministry immediately and move out of his parents' basement. But clarity about purpose is insufficient; process clarity is also essential.

Just as a process for constructing Grand Central Station was essential, a clearly defined process is essential in student ministry. Or the statement is simply a wish list and not a plan of action that guides the ministry.

A statement with no plan for execution is similar to an army general who places a map of a city to be conquered on the wall but never shares how the conquering will take place. The troops would love to conquer the city, but without a plan, nothing happens.

Eventually the troops will assume the city isn't worth conquering. The whole plan must have been flawed because direction was lacking as to *how* the conquering should take place.

While some student ministries possess a clear *what*, very few have a clear *how*.

How is your student ministry structured to produce life transformation in students? *How* do all the programs come together to move students toward spiritual maturity? *How* does all that your student ministry offers fit together to take students somewhere spiritually, to realize the *what* you have defined?

Please realize that we are not advocating yet another statement. Perhaps you already have too many. The number of statements leaders are encouraged to develop can be staggering: mission statement, vision statement, strategic statement, purpose statement, values statement, and so on.

The last thing our student ministries need is just another statement without a change in thinking. We need a fundamental shift in how we view our ministries, in how we operate. Hopefully you will allow God to give you clarity in both your purpose and process so that your purpose and process will be one in the same.

We advocate one overarching statement that defines *what* your ministry is about and *how* your ministry will make disciples. In other words, your purpose should be a process.

For clear understanding of your process, you must define, illustrate, measure, and communicate. These four aspects of clarity are crucial in creating a great blueprint.

Define Your Process

Defining your process is the most essential aspect of a simple student ministry. Without a clearly defined process, you will not know what to eliminate (focus), what process you are moving students through (movement), or what to unite your leadership team around (alignment). The importance of defining your process mandates the necessity of prayer and wrestling with discipleship through a biblical framework.

Defining your process must be a spiritual journey with God.

But get started. Don't slow momentum by excessive waiting. Student ministries have perfected the art of "tabling" an idea until it's forgotten or beaten-up so many times, no one wants to listen anymore.

But where do you begin?

First, discuss what type of student disciple you pray and hope your student ministry produces. The starting point is the end result, the mental picture of what you desire to build.

After you have invested time with God in prayer and sense His direction, begin the discussion and dreaming. If we were meeting with your student ministry leadership team for a consultation, we would use a dry erase board and write out the important aspects of discipleship for your student ministry.

We would begin with questions like: What type of student do you want your student ministry to make? What do you want your students to be? What would their lives look like? So right now, write down some of your initial responses to those questions.

While the list will vary in length, often the following phrases emerge:

- Worship God openly and intimately
- Develop a prayerful relationship with God
- Study the Scriptures
- Humbly place others above themselves
- Love people who are not believers
- Make wise choices based on the Word of God
- Embrace biblical community
- Share faith with others
- Possess heart for the world
- Know their spiritual gifts
- Serve others

At this point in a consultation, we would encourage your student ministry team to narrow the list as much as possible. Because the longer the list, the longer your student ministry process will be. And the longer the process, the less likely students will be able to progress through your process.

To narrow the list of *what* kind of student disciple, look for redundancy in your list. And look for aspects of discipleship that can be combined under one overarching phrase. For example, using the list above, we would encourage the student ministry leadership team to combine *serve others*, *know their spiritual gifts*, and *humbly place others above themselves* into one overarching phrase.

We suggest three to four key words or phrases as an ideal framework for defining a discipleship process in your student ministry. Once you believe you have defined *what* type of student disciple your ministry is going to make, you are ready to move to the next phase of defining your process.

Second, combine your phrases together into a process. Place the *what* phrases in key order, in process language. Do so, not based on how the phrases best sound together, but on *how* you believe spiritual growth best happens. Order the phrases, using your understanding of how Scripture describes spiritual growth.

In essence, you are marrying your purpose (what) and your process (how). Your purpose for existence and how you will disciple students will become one essential statement.

The middle school ministry, Emerge, at First Baptist Church of Oviedo, Florida, combined their purpose and process into one simple statement: *Middle school students will emerge into culture changers by being exposed to Jesus, being equipped to follow Jesus, and experiencing life serving Jesus.*

The statement is both the purpose and process of the student ministry. The student ministry wants to see students exposed relationally to Christ, trained to walk with Him, and dedicated to serving Him. And the ministry team describes this purpose as a process, with the phrases placed in strategic order.

The student ministry of Christ Fellowship in Miami, Florida, has the same process as the entire Christ Fellowship family. The student ministry seeks to connect students to God, others, ministry, and the world. Discipleship is defined as students who are growing in their relationship with God (connect to God), live in biblical community with other Christians (connect to others), know and use their spiritual gifts in service (connect to ministry), and live on mission in Miami and around the world (connect to the world).

And the purpose is described as a process because the order is essential. Students first connect to God in relationship before connecting to others in authentic community. And when a student is connected to both God and others, the response in that student will be to serve others (connect to ministry).

We are not suggesting that your process is the only way in which God works. Your process is a strategy and a blueprint. It is not a box in which God is confined. Now that you have placed the essential words or phrases describing discipleship into a sequential process, you are ready for the next step in defining your process.

Third, place weekly programs along your process. Perhaps you are one of those deeply spiritually reflective persons who insist on never blending discussion about programs with discussion about spiritual growth or discipleship. If so, you really have two choices. You can cancel all your programs or you can continue to run all your programs with the frustrating belief that they are completely useless.

For the rest of us, we would like to use our programs strategically to help bring students through the process of discipleship that God has given our student ministries. We know that students will come to our weekly programs so we desire to use those programs strategically. Just as we encourage you to marry your purpose and process into one statement, we challenge you to connect your programs to your ministry process. In other words, view your programs as tools to help students progress through your process.

In chapter 1, we discussed the transformation of Moses. Moses would meet with God on the mountain and God would transform him. Moses did not transform himself. God did the transforming. But Moses did place himself in the position to be transformed.

Growing up in the New Orleans area, I (Eric) would often ski or kneeboard in the bayous close to my house. The water is placid and perfect for skiing. You just have to watch out for the snakes and gators. When kneeboarding, I was simply along for the ride. The boat was doing the work, the pulling. But I needed to place myself in the best position to be pulled by the boat.

Transformation occurs in the same manner. Transformation is the work of the Holy Spirit, but we must place ourselves in the right position to be transformed.

Placing programs along your process should be viewed as placing opportunities for students to encounter God. If we were offering a consultation on this important aspect of defining your process, we would pose the questions: *What is the best environment for spiritual transformation to happen at each stage in your process? What is the best program you can offer for each stage of your process?*

If a program is not the best environment to place a student for spiritual transformation to occur, then don't utilize that weekly program in your process. Or the nonessential program will distract from what you believe are the best environments for students to encounter the transforming presence of God.

For example, Emerge, at First Baptist Church of Oviedo, utilizes a student worship service to *expose* students to Christ, Bible Fellowship groups to *equip* students, and student ministry teams to provide ministry opportunities for students to *experience* Christ through serving. Emerge's programs are connected to its process. Better stated, its programs are tools to move students through the process.

The student ministry of Christ Fellowship utilizes a student worship service to place students in the best environment to connect to God, small groups to place students in the best environment to connect with others, ministry teams to help students connect to a ministry, and mission projects as the best environment for students to connect to their world.

Do not change anything. Not yet. We will discuss eliminating nonessential programs later in the book. Simply discuss which programs are the best environments and commit to funnel your best energy and resources to those. Place one essential program for each phase of your process and utilize that program to help ensure a specific aspect of discipleship occurs in the lives of your students.

And once you've defined your process, illustrate your process.

Illustrate Your Process

Nike is well-known for its swoosh logo. Simple and easy to remember, the swoosh helps people identify with the product. Caroline Davidson, a Portland State University student, created the logo for $35 in 1971. She should have negotiated some sort of royalties within her contract.[3]

Apple Inc. designed its logo using an apple with a bite out of the right side. The original logo depicted a man eating an apple under a tree. The logo was too complex. To simplify, Apple opted for the single apple with the colors of the rainbow inverted. Further revision now has the Apple as a single color with a recognizable bite.

There are many ways to illustrate your process. Student ministries with simple processes use images such as a baseball diamond, a triangle, or a metaphor like the "foyer to the kitchen" (from Northpoint Church in Alpharetta, Georgia). The greatest characteristics of your illustration should be the clarity that the image provides and the message of movement and progression.

Your illustration should be closely connected with your process. If your process has three phases, then your illustration should communicate the three phases of your process.

The student ministry of Crossroads Community Church in Simpsonville, South Carolina, has a great design. Its process is *encountering God, connecting to others, and serving their world.*

The design for illustrating the process is simple and communicates movement.

Illustrating your process will add a visual perspective. Students will know their place in the process and know their "next step" by simply viewing the illustration.

We are visual people, and the illustration reinforces the meaning of the process. Specifically in the culture of teenagers, being visual is wise because students are bombarded with visual messages in every other aspect of their lives. And communication with visual stimulation always increases retention.

Illustrate your process. And measure your process.

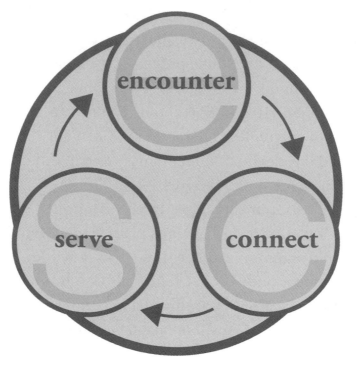

Used by permission.

Measure Your Process

An accurate measurement can mean life or death when determining the distance of a bungee jump. Effective measuring means a great deal to the football team waiting for the first-down call or the call of a turnover to end the game. An appropriate measure can tell if those shorts you are wearing are the right length or if they border on obscene.

Measuring is essential.

While measuring can be a painful reminder that ministry has not changed in the past year, ignoring numbers keeps us from facing reality. And prevents us from healthy discussion and evaluation.

Most student ministries measure something. Some measure attendance at the pet program of the student pastor. Others measure attendance at the program that's most essential to the senior pastor or another supervising staff member.

While we agree that measurement is important, we challenge student ministry leaders to view numbers horizontally and not vertically. Viewing numbers vertically is viewing them through the lens of a program. *Do we have the same number of students attending this program as we did last year?*

Viewing numbers horizontally is viewing numbers through the lens of your process. *Are we moving students proportionally from program to program within our process?*

To measure horizontally, attendance must be measured at each stage in your process. The data represents how your ministry, as a whole, is moving students to greater levels of commitment. The data helps you notice holes in your ministry process and respond accordingly.

Let us be painfully transparent here. We measure the student ministry at Christ Fellowship, Miami, horizontally; therefore, we measure how many students are attending a worship service (connect to God), how many students are plugged into small groups (connect to others), how many students serve (connect to ministry), and how many students engage in missions (connect to the world).

Quarterly, we evaluate. A recent quarterly report looked similar to the chart below (this is a scaled-down version).

Weekend (God)	Small Groups (Others)	Serve (Ministry)	Missions (World)
25 percent increase	6 percent increase	19 percent increase	18 percent increase

Do you see a hole?

If we measured *vertically*, we would be excited about our small-group attendance in our student ministry. We are growing!

But because we view our numbers *horizontally*, through the lens of our process, we realized that we were not effectively moving the new students from the weekend to our small groups. And the report forced us to engage in healthy discussion and ramp up communication to students about our small-group opportunities.

A Global Positioning System (GPS) is analogous to measuring the process. After determining where you want to go, enter the coordinates and the GPS will show you how to get there.

The GPS tracks your progress. The roads you have driven, drive time, and maximum speed are all accounted for by satellite. The GPS is an objective way of showing where you are going and the distance you have covered.

Similarly, when numbers are viewed horizontally, there is a clear picture of movement (or lack of movement) through the process.

Define your process. Illustrate your process. Measure it. And communicate it.

Communicate Your Process

When boaters come to Miami, they learn very quickly that the ocean channel markers are important. The channels in the Miami area are deep enough for a boat to pass through, but often the edges of those channels are shallow and rocky and can damage a propeller or leave a boater beached.

These markers are the red and green signs on the sides of each channel that show where travel is safe. On smaller and more obscure waterways, the channel markers may only be sticks in the sand. As long as the captain can see where the markers are, he can navigate the journey.

After a hurricane, however, some of these channel markers are missing. Or sometimes a boat with a novice at the wheel will take out a channel marker or two. When channel markers are missing, there is confusion about which direction is correct. Someone may make a decision to steer where he normally wouldn't because a marker is missing.

You can quickly find yourself in a dangerous predicament.

As a leader, you must point out the markers to your leaders and students. You must effectively communicate the process God has given your student ministry. If you don't, there will be directional confusion. And the lack of clarity can lead your student ministry into a dangerously ineffective season of ministry.

Since students move through the process of spiritual transformation relationally under the nurture and care of godly leaders, communication with leadership is essential.

Leadership must own the process passionately. They cannot simply rent or borrow your vision. They must own the student ministry vision themselves. Regular and constant communication is vital.

Rally your team around the process often.

Celebrate with your leaders stories of students who are moving through the process. Connect the value of each phase in the process to the growth in their lives.

Invite a key leader occasionally to share why the process is important to him. The process will be reinforced and sound fresh coming from someone other than you.

When a new idea surfaces, ask questions corporately. *Does the program fit? How will this help move students along in the journey? Are we stepping outside the vision God gave us with this new idea?* Questions discussed openly answer questions that weren't asked and reinforce the commitment of the student ministry to what really is essential.

Give leadership a process quiz.

Create an illustration of the process with blanks for your team to answer. Don't make the quiz a pass-or-fail issue, but stress the importance of the leaders' influence on students and how that relates to the process. Give the quiz often in the beginning stages. Repeat the quiz as often as you feel necessary. Or if you e-mail your leaders often, include a question about the process for fun. Give the first correct responder a small gift.

Communicating your student ministry discipleship process is not a one-time event. Many discussions must take place. Very few people hear something once and go all-out. Implementing a process is . . . a process.

While communication to leadership is vital, so is communication to the students. Understanding always precedes commitment. For your students to move through the process of discipleship in your student ministry, they must first understand and embrace it. When students understand the process, they move through the process and bring their friends with them. Great communication is required in a variety of settings.

Share the process in large-group settings.

Large groups offer the luxury of speaking to everyone at one time. When teaching students, occasionally weave the process into your talk. Articulate the process in relationship to their spiritual growth. Illustrate the practicality of the programs that your student ministry offers.

Share the process in small-group settings.

Some of your most powerful lessons will be shared spontaneously from your heart. As you meet with students in everyday discussion, share real stories of life change. Celebrate what God is doing on a personal level and how He has used the process of discipleship in *your* life.

Authentically live out the process.

Your loudest sermon will be your life. Especially with students. The clearest form of communication to others will be how you live on a personal level. You must do personally what you are asking students to do.

If you tell students that small groups are vital to spiritual growth, you should be in a small group. If your process includes missions, be on mission. Don't just lead a trip somewhere. Share your faith with people in your life.

When you live out the reality of your ministry process, you are qualified to speak from experience. You are able to share what God taught you in your small group. The story of you sharing your faith will be fresh and new and not a recycled illustration from last year's mission trip.

Define, illustrate, measure, and communicate your process. But above all, live out your process.

DISCUSSION QUESTIONS

1. Is our current vision statement being brought to life, or is it more of a wish list?
2. What type of student do we want to spiritually produce?
3. Can we discuss discipleship in process language? Do we possess a clear *how*?
4. Do our current weekly programs place students in the best environment for life change?
5. Do we have any way of measuring the effectiveness of our discipleship process? If so, how could we make some measurement changes?
6. Are we, as leaders, living out what we desire our students to become?

CHAPTER FOUR

Movement

Nothing happens until something moves.

—Albert Einstein

Dell has shattered the warehouse myth. Some companies love big warehouses. They feel safe with lots of inventory on big shelves in big warehouses, always ready for that next big order. They feel as if they will always be able to meet customer demands and customer expectations. Dell disagrees. It does not want its resources on the shelves.

In the technology business, the product loses value on the shelves. So Dell only keeps two hours of inventory. Which means that if you order a PC on dell.com, the parts will not arrive to Dell until two hours before your PC is shipped to you.

Dell wants its resources on the street, not in the warehouse. Thus Dell has designed a very strategic process to move its best resources to the street as quickly as possible.[1]

Sadly many churches and student ministries still believe in the warehouse myth. They build big warehouses and shelve a bunch of Christians. They keep students in the warehouse, on the shelves. The warehouse feels safe.

Complicated student ministries become warehouses for students to attend a multitude of programs and never live out their faith on the street. A student ministry becomes a warehouse when students get more addicted to the programming offered in the warehouse than living out their faith.

Perhaps the warehouse myth needs to be busted in your context.

Time for Change

Programming is changing at Willow Creek Community Church.

In 2007 Willow Creek released findings from a multiple-year study of its ministry. The reason for the study was a commendable desire to know which programs and activities were helping people move forward spiritually. The data, Senior Pastor Bill Hybels said, was "earth shaking, ground breaking, and mind blowing." He continued:

Some of the stuff that we have put millions of dollars into thinking it would really help our people grow and develop spiritually, when the data actually came back it wasn't helping people that much. Other things that we didn't put that much money into and didn't put much staff against is stuff our people are crying out for . . . We made a mistake. What we should have done when people crossed the line of faith and become Christians, we should have started telling people and teaching people that they have to take responsibility to become "self feeders." We should have gotten people, taught people, how to read their Bible between service, how to do the spiritual practices much more aggressively on their own.[2]

Willow Creek was willing to admit its programs were not moving people along in their spiritual lives. While some people used Hybels's statement to bash the style of ministry at Willow Creek, we applaud any leadership team who is willing to initiate changes that will result in moving people toward spiritual maturity more effectively.

And a packed calendar never guarantees spiritual movement. Attendance at multiple programs has never been a true gauge of the love a student has for Jesus.

If programs only move students around inside the warehouse, ministry becomes a spiritual parking lot. Faith becomes equated with *being at church* and soon both of them become routine. Thus, for many students, there is little differentiation between faith in God and being present at youth group.

Students with routine faith are everywhere.

And to combat the routine faith in the lives of our students, our programming must be designed to nudge students along in their journey and equip them to grow apart from our student ministry programming.

Programs, when created strategically and properly sequenced, serve as a catalyst for learning spiritual disciplines. According to our research, student ministries that utilized a discipleship process embedded training within their process to encourage spiritual disciplines away from the student ministry.

These student ministries included corporate worship and teaching as learning tools. Community, accountability, and spiritual disciplines were reinforced through some type of small-group interaction. And all the student ministries highlighted via the case studies utilize a service and/or mission experience to move students to a point of service.

Thinking Theologically about Programs

If we offer programs in our student ministries (and we all do), there must be an underlying theology behind the programs. Otherwise, we truly are event planners, travel agents, or program managers. Programs must be used as tools to place students in the pathway for true transformation.

The apostle Paul wrote about spiritual transformation in two crucial verses in his letter to the church at Philippi:

> So then, my dear friends, just as you have always obeyed, not only in my presence, but now even more in my absence, work out your own salvation with fear and trembling. For it is God who is working in you, enabling you both to will and to act for His good purpose. (Phil. 2:12–13)

There is a tension in the verses, isn't there?

The phrase "work out your own salvation" seems to put responsibility for spiritual transformation on us. Yet the next verse clearly says that God is the one who enables spiritual transformation to occur.

How is the tension resolved?

Spiritual transformation is a divine-human partnership. God is the one who grows us, but we must place ourselves in the position to be transformed.[3]

The classic book *Celebration of Discipline*, by Richard Foster, challenges believers to engage in spiritual disciplines. Yet Foster is clear in the early parts of his book that the spiritual disciplines do not transform us. Prayer, study, and fasting do not bring about transformation. God does. But the disciplines do put us in the pathway for us to be transformed by God.[4]

If we think about spiritual disciplines as tools that put us in the pathway of God's transformation, can we not think of our programs in the same manner?

Several times in the Gospels people were either brought to or placed themselves in a position to be changed by Jesus. Intentional steps were made to experience transformation that was not possible on their own.

In Mark 2, four guys were strategic in helping their friend get to Jesus. The friend was paralyzed, and these four guys were willing to do anything to see him healed. However, Jesus was teaching in a house that was standing room only. Their creativity led them to carry their buddy to a rooftop and remove a portion of the roof where Jesus was teaching.

After being placed near Jesus, the paralytic's life was never the same. Jesus completely healed him.

The friends did whatever possible to get the paralytic to Jesus, knowing that if their friend could get close enough, his life would be changed forever.

In Mark 5, a woman suffering from a hemorrhage made her way to the feet of Jesus. No one had been able to cure this woman's problem; she was completely out of options. She traveled alone and knew her only shot at healing rested in Jesus.

She quietly made her way through the noisy crowd. Despite the huge number of people and the possible embarrassment, she subtly touched the garment of Jesus. Immediately the pain left and the bleeding stopped. Twelve years of agony were over. She was in the right place to experience transformation.

These stories share a similar truth. Change happens when people (students) are placed in situations where growth (and healing) can begin.

Programming should always point students to Jesus. We know that when students can experience Jesus, their lives are changed forever. Moving students through the programs in your process should be moving them to the best places for God to bring transformation. Moving students through your process with different opportunities for growth will help fulfill the call God has given you to disciple students.

If you want to move students through your process, you must program strategically, program sequentially, and move students intentionally.

Program Strategically

Wise leaders strategically place their programs along the process that God has given their ministry. They carefully examine their programs and refuse to offer a program or event merely from routine.

Radiate, the high school ministry of Grace Baptist Church in Cedarville, Ohio, has programs that engage students in a simple discipleship process. Radiate implements what it calls the *G3 Philosophy of Ministry: Gospel* (Evangelism), *Grow* (Discipleship), and *Go* (Service).

Each weekly program offered is created specifically for a purpose and sequentially moves students deeper into discipleship. The weekly programming consists of three programs as aligned with their process.

Radiate (Gospel) is the Wednesday night entry-level service for high school students. The atmosphere is high energy, and student friendly and includes a clear gospel message. Students invite their friends to Radiate and guests often visit. Because the student ministry places a high value on relationships, adult leaders are recruited to build relationships with the students.

After Radiate, students are encouraged to attend a Sunday morning teaching program. This program is designed to help students understand deeper truths of the Bible.

Students are encouraged to attend Radiate (Gospel), attend the teaching environment (Grow), and get involved in serving others (Go). Serving others consists of service projects, serving on a ministry team, or going on a mission trip. In either capacity, students are encouraged to live what they have been learning in the previous phases of the process.

Radiate moves students in a sequential order. For your process to be successfully executed, you must match your programs to your process both strategically and sequentially.

Begin with your clearly defined process.

Strategic programming begins with your process. Do not view your programs as your place to start; that will lead to clutter and confusion.

You will lose the integrity of your process if you design a process around your existing programming. Altering your process to fit the system of your programs would prove your programs have become the chief reason your student ministry exists.

Choose one program for each phase.

As we meet with ministry leaders, we notice an obvious tendency to stack multiple programs in the early phases of the discipleship process. Well-intended leaders mistakenly believe that another program will enhance the process.

In reality, multiple layers of programming for one phase of the process holds students in the early phases of the process. Multiple programs for one phase of the process keeps students on the shelves in the warehouse.

Students have only so much available time to participate in the programs your student ministry offers. If you offer multiple programs at the early stages in your process, the students will not have time to move to the later stages in your discipleship process.

Furthermore, more than one program per phase of the process ultimately divides energy and focus. Promoting, explaining, financing, and staffing an extra program that serves the same function as another program are wasteful and drive the level of excellence down for all your programs.

Movement is increased when there is only one program for each phase of your process because the students clearly know the next step.

Design each program for a specific phase.

As you place programs along your process, be sure that each program is designed uniquely for the specific point in the process.

Take time to develop each program. Think through what each program should look like in order to fulfill a specific phase of your discipleship process.

For example, if you determine that small groups are part of your process and you design a small-group program, protect that program from morphing into a different existing program. A godly, good-hearted person may suggest that you design your groups similar to the large-group meeting, but the morphing would create redundancy in your programming. And students would be robbed of the group experience you first envisioned.

Protect your programs like a fat guy protects a box of doughnuts, like a receiver protects the football . . . you get the idea.

Program Sequentially

Learning to free dive requires sequential learning. Free diving is done on a single breath of air with no tanks, no tubes, and no oxygen of any kind.

Beginning free divers are snorkelers. These people are comfortable swimming on or near the surface of the water. Expert free divers can reach depths of one hundred feet. Competitive free divers dive to five hundred feet deep or more. Crazy.

Whether you are free diving down to twenty feet or eighty feet, you must know and understand your limitations and how to respond to various depths.

A person who has never been diving before isn't taken to eighty-foot depths of the ocean and dropped overboard. Unless, of course, the person has crossed the wrong people and the guy throwing him overboard is named Big Tony or Joey Bag of Doughnuts.

Diving to great depths isn't a starting point. Free divers don't dive to eighty feet until time is spent learning how to handle the pressures and complexities of diving at shallower depths. Deep-water dives don't happen until the diver is confident with the shallow-water dives.

The shallow water is the beginning. The deep water is the goal.

The apostle Peter understood sequence in terms of growing spiritually. Peter gave a command for those who

are young in the faith to "crave pure spiritual milk, so that
. . . you may grow up in your salvation" (1 Pet. 2:2 NIV).

Babies don't eat steak for their first few years. Steak
tastes great and has a lot of protein but is too much at this
stage of development. Babies begin with milk. A short time
later the child begins to eat the flavorful goop in little jars
and moves on successively. As growth continues, babies'
food changes in order to meet their growing needs.

Different steps are also required at different stages of
spiritual growth. Your programming must be sequential for
students to be moved to a deeper level. The sequence of your
programs should match the sequence of your process.

Order the sequence to reflect your process.

There should be a tight marriage between your purpose,
process, and programming. Students should be able to
see how each program fleshes out that phase in the
process. When the order of your programs matches your
process, you make the steps clear to students.

Student Community, the student ministry of Community Christian Church in the Chicagoland area, offers programs that are designed to move students deeper. Student
Community lives out the process of the three Cs: *Celebrate,
Connect,* and *Contribute.*

Celebrate is the first phase of the process. The Celebrate
service consists of great music, relevant teachings from the
Bible, and time to build relationships. Both corporate and

personal, students are invited to celebrate their relationship with God and invite their friends to do the same.

Connect programming is designed to focus on building biblical community. Small groups are used to facilitate deeper discussion and accountability and to reinforce the teaching from the weekend Celebrate service.

Contribute is the last phase. Students are encouraged to serve either in the student ministry or another ministry in the church. Students serve in the greeting ministry, the band, the parking lot, etc. Student Community also partners with community groups to meet the needs of people in their area. Ultimately the goal is to create servant-hearted students.

Student Community's sequence makes sense: "Student Communities' process makes sense. Students are moved to the next natural step of discipleship. Each step moves students toward the goal of becoming servant-hearted."

Movement in "bite-sized" chunks that allow students to grow is possible through sequential programming. Students can move forward when the next level of programming makes sense. As students move through the programs prayerfully, so does their growth in intimacy with Christ.

Create a clear entry point.

Your process should begin with a program that's open to students who are at any place in their spiritual journey. From that program, each step in the process should be another level of refinement to create a place for students to be further transformed.

The entry point is the front door to your ministry. Leaders of simple student ministry know there must be one program that's open for every student, regardless if the student is a growing Christian or a guest for the very first time.

Everyone is invited to come to this program. This is the program for students to come and get to know your ministry. Guests most likely come, and friends are usually invited to this program.

This program is typically the largest of the few programs you will have. Compared to the other programs that lead deeper into discipleship, this program requires the least amount of commitment.

Identify the next levels of programming.

Clearly identifying the next phase of discipleship for your students is very important. The entry point has been defined, but what should a student do next?

With each progressing program, the level of commitment should grow. Discipleship is costly. Subsequently, as the commitment level grows, the number of people who participate in the next level of discipleship decreases.

Once all programs have been strategically and sequentially placed, the challenge is to begin moving students through the process. All of the work of placing programs in incremental growth stages along your process was done so that movement can be as fluid as possible.

Move Intentionally

If you have ever taken a road trip more than six hours in length with students, then you understand intentional movement. As a leader, you know the goal is arriving at the desired location. Distraction looms as long bathroom breaks threaten to delay the trip.

Most leaders in student ministry have their own set of rules for road trips. Some rules are for safety, others are to make sure nobody is making out, and yet another set of rules is to keep the trip moving forward.

When you road trip, whether you are taking a bus or caravanning with seven minivans, leaders apply many of the same unwritten rules. For the hard-core road trippers, these aren't suggestions, but rather valuable student ministry truths that save precious time.

- Everyone should eat, hit the restrooms, and fuel up the vehicles at the same stop.
- Do not wait until time to leave the gas station to get in line to buy your food.
- If the girls' bathroom line is backed up, start using the guys' bathroom. There's never anyone in there anyway! Somebody else guard the door. And spray some Febreze!
- Do a head count after everyone is back in the vehicles; make sure no one gets left behind. Going back for students is the big time waster.

These simple rules represent intentional movement. Every stop along the way isn't the final destination, so continual movement (prodding) of students is necessary. There are distractions that hinder progress, so focus is a must.

Leaders are intentional on road trips because they know there is a better place to be than a gas station in Nowhereville. Encouragements and clear direction are necessary to save valuable time getting to your destination.

Movement is a good idea on road trips, but a student's spiritual life also needs encouragement to move on.

Student ministries can get distracted, and students can be in the same place spiritually for years, so, they are chilling out spiritually somewhere on the road to discipleship Nowhereville, waiting for whatever and whenever. Simple student ministries find creative ways to move students along on the process of discipleship. Here are some suggestions to get students moving.

Follow up on guests.

How do you follow up on students who visit your ministry? Do you have a system in place? Or do you just hope guests will find their way into points of connection in your ministry? If a student doesn't feel as though anyone knows he was there, he will have difficulty making a connection.

If a nonbelieving guest visits, the ramifications are far more reaching. Suppose a student is searching for God and comes to your ministry to find out more about Him. Every aspect of the visit will either point him to God or away from God. If the people who claim to love and follow God couldn't care less about the student's presence, their apathy is a poor reflection on God's heart for people.

If guests aren't followed up on in your student ministry, change the paradigm. Right now.

In order to attach guests to your ministry, the first step is to follow up with a letter, phone call, or visit. Make guests feel welcome, but please don't embarrass them in the process.

Capitalize on relationships.

Relationships are the connectors for students to your ministry. Students' relationships are very influential in their lives. Students not only care about the *what*, but also the *who . . . who else is going to be there?*

Students are motivated to move when someone is moving with them. Very few students will try something new alone. A new place is difficult to experience when you are with people you don't know.

However, relationships can bridge the gap between dormancy and spiritual growth. A student will visit a ministry because a friend invited him. A student will listen to his friend talk about how Jesus changed his life.

Students won't move forward in your process because it's written on the Web site. Students will not take the next step of discipleship because of the writing on the student room's wall.

Students will check out the next phase of discipleship if someone cares about them enough to ask them. Students will be more open to spiritual things if a friend or caring leader is there with them.

For example, to move students to a group (ABF, Area Bible Fellowship), Sunday school, small groups, or whatever you call your group structure), here are some simple suggestions we have observed:

Simple step 1: Encourage students who attend a group to invite students from the entry-level program to the next step. Not only do retention rates rise when the invitation is from a friend, but students also learn how to walk with others through the student ministry process.

Simple step 2: Set up a booth manned with volunteer group leaders ready to answer questions from students. Provide necessary information such as time, location, leader, etc. The leaders would also be able to introduce other students who belong to that particular small group.

Simple step 3: Encourage group leaders to be part of your entry-point program. As leaders invest their lives into students, inviting students to join them in their group will come naturally.

Notice that each step has less to do with information and more to do with relationship. An invitation from a friend or leader carries much more weight than writing on a wall.

Continually ask, "Now what?"

A growing student won't feel comfortable in the same place very long. Students who are maturing want to be challenged and experience their faith. The Holy Spirit is maturing them and shaping them. Thus, they have a hunger for more.

Asking, *Now what?* puts us in the shoes of the student. *Where do I go from here? How do I grow?* When we begin to envision what's next for the students, we can create transitions that will facilitate movement.

Howard Levanthal, a social psychologist from Yale University, led an interesting experiment in the 1960s that provided a powerful argument for showing people their next step.[5]

Levanthal purposed to convince college seniors at Yale to get immunized with a tetanus shot. As part of the experiment, he passed out seven-page booklets about the importance of inoculation and the dangers of tetanus.

The booklets came in "high-fear" versions and "low-fear" versions in order to test how students would respond to the advertisement. The campus health center was offering free tetanus shots so the excuses for not getting one would be minimal.

The pamphlets simply stressed the importance of receiving a tetanus shot.

After a month of experimentation, a disappointing 3 percent of seniors showed up for a tetanus shot. Neither low-fear nor high-fear persuasion booklets effectively motivated students to get the shot.

Sometime later Levanthal repeated the experiment, but this version of the booklet included a map of the campus with the health center circled and the times shots would be provided.

After gathering the results, Levanthal found that 28 percent of students received the vaccination.

The result between the two tests is significant. The difference is found in clarity of the next step. *The clinic exists. It's located here. Here are the times.*

Leaders in student ministry must also create small bridges that encourage movement between programs. Consider which obstacles may be keeping students from moving: program times, location, understanding, etc., and work to dismantle the obstructions.

Create a clear step for newbies.

Jeff and his wife Jen, who don't have children of their own yet, recently became foster parents. The plan was to foster one child at a time in order to "ease" into parenthood. However, when the call came to foster, a brother and a sister were offered and splitting them up wasn't a good idea.

Foster parents are desperately needed in Miami, where Jeff and Jen live. Children all over the county are left parentless because of neglect, death, or imprisonment.

Children are left alone and are often at the mercy of the courts; sometimes they grow up and spend their formative years in a group home. Many have no family to care for them or to meet their needs. There is no sense of belonging or identity; the abandoned must learn to provide for themselves.

Student ministries often take the same, unexplainable approach to new believers. In many cases, new Christians may be called to the front, asked to stand, and maybe even cheered for. There is excitement for a few minutes and possibly a high five or a side hug. And often discipleship ends at that point.

Many student ministries passionately preach the Great Commission (Matt. 28:19–20). The emphasis, however, is almost always on the "make disciples" portion of the Scripture.

We agree that we are to make disciples. We are passionate to see students transformed by Jesus. But the command does not end there.

The tragedy is the inadvertent (or overt) neglect of the next few words.

> Then Jesus came near and said to them, "All authority has been given to Me in heaven and on earth. Go, therefore, and make disciples of all nations, baptizing them in the name of the Father and of the Son and of the Holy Spirit, teaching them to observe everything I have commanded you. And remember, I am with you always, to the end of the age." (Matt. 28:18–20)

Teaching them to observe everything I have commanded you.

In context, "Make disciples, then disciple them!"

Acts 2 gives a short synopsis of how the early church discipled new believers. Peter had addressed a large crowd and three thousand were converted to the faith. These new Christians were included in a new way of life.

> And they devoted themselves to the apostles' teaching, to fellowship, to the breaking of bread, and to prayers. Then fear came over everyone, and many wonders and signs were being performed through the apostles. Now all the believers were together and had everything in common. (Acts 2:42–44)

New believers were assimilated into the lives of other Christians. Listening to biblical teaching, fellowship, praying, and living life together were phenomenal means of discipling the new converts.

The believers in Acts did a great job of discipleship. The Christians understood that new believers are people who matter to God. As a newborn baby must receive care and guidance to survive, so must the new Christian. The new Christian will not survive spiritually by himself.

Help students understand the importance of their decision for Christ and the impact on their life now and in eternity. Teach them the importance of spiritual disciplines and the need for daily connection to God apart from a ministry program. Connect students to the next level of discipleship in your ministry so growth can continue.

Refuse to produce spiritual orphans by getting new student believers grounded spiritually and plugged into the process God has given you.

Move students to mission.

The Dead Sea is a unique body of water. The water is so salty that nothing but bacteria lives in it. No fish, no plant life, nothing. The water is far too salty to sustain life. The water is so salty that it makes humans more buoyant. Tourists love taking pictures of themselves floating on top of the water and, unfortunately, showing those pictures to their friends on arrival at home.

What's crazy is that fresh, living water flows into the Dead Sea from rivers that are normal and sustain life. After emptying into the Dead Sea, the once vibrant water becomes salty and loses life.

The Dead Sea isn't disgusting because of the input. Just the opposite; it is dead because there is no output. There are no rivers or tributaries taking water out of the Dead Sea. Plenty of fresh water flows in, but with no outlets, it gets salty and funky. Only stale, gross, salty water remains.

And it dies.

Student ministries pour into students but often make the mistake of not moving them to mission. Activities aren't missions. Conferences aren't being on mission. Fundraisers don't make the cut either.

Teaching about evangelism and the importance of sharing Jesus with no tangible experience to live it out is a Dead

Sea philosophy. Great truth goes in, but there is no practical application to take the truth outside the church walls.

Moving students to mission doesn't mean everyone has to get a passport and learn to speak Chinese. (Although that would be awesome!) Mission doesn't necessarily mean you must drive for hours somewhere to put into practice what has been heard. Consider these phases of moving students to missions.

Go local.

Implement missions in your neighborhood.

Many student ministries wait for students to come to the church to share Jesus with them. However, when we look at the life of Jesus, we see a completely different approach to loving the lost (see Luke 15:1). An approach that is desperately needed in student ministry. Jesus lived His life among the people.

Encourage students to live missionally. Your students are the best resource to share Jesus with their friends. Empower them to lead a group on their school campus that is serious about winning their friends to Jesus. Don't just tell them about being a witness at school; provide a means for them to live it out.

There are other small mission steps students can experience and impact their community at the same time.

Host a barbecue at a home for displaced children and have students play football with the residents. Hand out bottles of ice water on a busy street. Offer to clean restrooms at a local restaurant for free. Adopt a nearby middle school or high school and serve them by painting or pressure washing the facilities and take the faculty breakfast with a thank-you note that says, "Thank you for teaching our students."

God uses students serving in their local communities in powerful ways. First, the community is the recipient of Christ followers being a blessing to the city. The church becomes a source of care for the people living in the area. Second, the students understand the responsibility of reaching their city. Missions is now understood as being even the person next door. Third, the bond that is created between students as they serve together only encourages their spiritual growth.

Go national/global.

Organize a mission trip either inside or outside of the United States. Organizing a mission trip is no small task. However, the rewards far outnumber the investment. Many students' lives have been changed forever because of a well thought out mission trip.

Here are a few ideas about involving your students on mission trips.

Travel to a place that has been affected by natural disaster or extreme poverty. Let your students experience being the hands and feet of Jesus by aiding people in dire need.

Don't stop at being a resource to the needy; share Jesus with them.

Teach your students that when you meet people's physical needs, you also have the opportunity to meet their spiritual needs. If a student only swings a hammer and isn't taught how that can relate to sharing Jesus, the point will be missed.

Partner with a missionary or a ministry in another country that could utilize the help of a team. Students will get to experience other cultures and God at work in the lives of other believers.

People learn best through experience, and this is especially true for teenagers.

Leading students on mission trips brings to life all the "you will be my witnesses" (Acts 1:8 NIV) talks they have heard. Students get to see God at work in different areas of the nation and the world. For the first time in their lives, students will be so uncomfortable that their faith goes to a new level.

When students understand why they are going and whom they are going to serve, missions come to life. No longer do they hear, *You should go*, but rather, *Here's where we're going, Here's how we're best used,* and *Here's the difference it will make in eternity.*

Missions are the experiences that breathe life into the teaching. Without these experiences, students simply get "spiritually bloated" and begin to lose life.

As you read this chapter, Dell was effectively moving computer parts to its warehouse. But Dell's best resources will not be in the warehouse much longer. Its best resources are being moved to the street.

As God brings students into your student ministry, will you effectively move them to places of spiritual transformation? Will you ultimately move them to the street where they can be salt and light in the culture in which God has placed them?

DISCUSSION QUESTIONS

1. Does our student ministry feel like a warehouse? Why?
2. What is the theology behind our programming?
3. Why does process focused instead of program focused make sense?
4. Are our weekly programs in sequence with our process?
5. How can we make the next steps in our ministry more clear to students?
6. What is our current plan for discipling new believers? Are we being effective with connecting them to our ministry?

CHAPTER FIVE

Alignment

> May the God who gives endurance and
> encouragement give you a spirit of unity among
> yourselves as you follow Christ Jesus, so that with
> one heart and mouth you may glorify the God and
> Father of our Lord Jesus Christ.
>
> —Romans 15:5–6 NIV

Because of alignment and phenomenal execution, twenty-four thousand people are still alive. More than twelve thousand people were rescued by air support and eleven thousand six hundred were evacuated by means on the ground. Hospital patients delivered to safety numbered nearly ninety-five hundred.

During the days following Hurricane Katrina, more than three hundred U.S. Coast Guard men and women poured in to the Gulf Coast from more than twenty different Coast Guard units across the country. In the face of tropical storm force winds and 100-degree heat, rescue swimmers worked tirelessly to pull people stranded on rooftops and liberate people clinging to trees for their lives.[1]

The story is personal as my (Eric) aunt and uncle were rescued from the water after floodwaters destroyed their home.

Flight and ground crews worked tirelessly to support the aircraft. Since the ultimate goal was saving lives, the crews courageously persevered through dehydration, dangerous predicaments, and long days of work with little or no rest.

No matter your view of the political scene surrounding Katrina, all would agree that the Coast Guard performed with excellence. It lived up to its motto, *Semper Paratus* (Always Ready).

The mission's success can be attributed to corporate alignment. The Coast Guard trains its people so that any pilot, navigator, or rescue swimmer can join any crew at any time and execute a mission. The deep commitment to alignment isn't exclusive to flight crews but also extends to ground support, flight controllers, and other aspects of the USCG.

In the case of Katrina, human lives were saved because of the Coast Guard's commitment to uniting personnel around the smallest details. The Coast Guard crews' willingness to put their individualism aside aligned them around their common goal: rescue people and save lives.

Alignment Begins with Unity

Alignment is the product of people unified around a common purpose. If student ministries are going to complete their mission and effectively reach students with the gospel, alignment is imperative. However, unity has been a problem for Christians and student ministries since the launch of the Christian faith. A quick scan through the letters to early churches reveals our ongoing struggle with unity.

Jesus experienced the disunity of those who were closest to Him. The disciples were great men committed to Jesus even to the point of giving their lives. In spite of their kingdom mind-set, two of the disciples had their own version of what the kingdom should look like.

James and John, two guys who were part of Jesus' inner circle, weren't vague about their desires. They went straight to Jesus and said, "We want you to do for us whatever we ask" (Mark 10:35 NIV).

Whoa.

Wait a minute. These two former nobodies approach the Creator of the universe and make demands? Can you imagine the guts required to put the muscle on the Almighty?

Their motivation for such a demand was their position in heaven. "Let one of us sit at your right and the other at your left in your glory" (Mark 10:37 NIV).

Since both were serving with Jesus on earth, why not have the best seats in heaven? If people were going to see

Jesus, James and John would be close by. Now that is some front row, center court seats!

Jesus quickly put James and John in their places. These two couldn't comprehend the gravity of their request. Jesus reminded both of them that they would suffer like He was going to suffer and gave them a short lesson on living the life of a servant (see Mark 10:41–45).

The Gospel of Mark says the other disciples became "indignant" with James and John because of their request. In our vernacular, Peter and the guys were about to go postal on James and John for asking for the best seats.

Selfish behavior and selfish mind-sets always produce disunity. Disunity, in return, destroys the alignment of a group of people who are on the same mission. No longer is everyone striving to accomplish the same mission, but rather his or her own version of what that mission should be.

People who are called to the same mission but act independently of each other aren't unified. Simply existing together or wearing the same student ministry shirts doesn't ensure alignment. Players can be on the same team but have completely different goals.

Jesus knew unity would be an issue so He prayed specifically for those of us who would follow Him.

> I pray also for those who will believe in me through their message, that all of them may be one, Father, just as you are in me and I am in you. May they also

be in us so that the world may believe that you have sent me. (John 17:20–21 NIV)

Jesus prayed that we would share the same heart, passion, and vision. He wants His heartbeat to be our heartbeat and His passion to be our passion. Jesus elevated unity to the status of the most effective evangelist tool by praying that our unity would be a testimony to those who don't believe.

When believers are unified, an unbelieving world is attracted. When Christians put their selfishness aside, Jesus is glorified. The team gets a mark in the win column. The mission is accomplished.

Unity is a catalyst for aligning the leaders on your team. But alignment must also be intentional.

Intentional Alignment

To be a rescue swimmer for the Coast Guard, you must first complete training that is similar in intensity to Green Berets' or Navy SEALs' training. A mere three hundred rescue swimmers exist throughout the Coast Guard. Only seventy-five candidates attempt to complete the school each year, and more than half drop out before ever getting in the water.[2]

The Coast Guard effectively attracts people who are serious about the mission. These recruits will jump out of a helicopter into thirty-foot waves on the Bering Sea because of their shared commitment to saving lives. The Coast Guard doesn't casually approach the issue of alignment. Too much is at stake. The USCG intentionally aligns people to its *what* (saving lives) and to its *how* (their strategy).

Student ministries typically have no idea *what* type of student they seek to produce, much less *how* the discipleship will be accomplished in that specific context. Different opinions and strategies are formed and chaos ensues.

The people you place in leadership are the difference between unity and chaos. If leaders are serious about seeing student's lives transformed by Jesus, they can be unified. These are the leaders that will be a picture of godliness to your students. These leaders will help usher students through the process of discipleship God has given your student ministry.

When building a great team, you must be intentional. You must recruit based on the process, unite your team around the process, offer accountability, implement the process everywhere, and continually align.

Recruit on the Process

Coast Guard rescue swimmers don't only swim. Swimmers must also provide emergency medical treatment for rescued individuals. Being comfortable in the water in the midst of stressful situations is also a necessity.

Swimming is only a small part of the bigger picture. Many would-be recruits are proficient swimmers but crack under stressful situations. Despite their swimming skills, they ultimately aren't right for the team.

Likewise, there is more to being a great student ministry team than merely a grouping of talented individuals. Talented teachers, discussion leaders, musicians, and administrators may be of great value, but if each person moves in his own direction, the team and, ultimately, the students suffer.

The defining aspect of your team should be the shared commitment to the simple process. Talent, abilities, and even passion must be secondary to unity. No amount of talent is worth dividing the energy and resources of the student ministry.

Let the talented and unwilling align somewhere else.

When sharing your discipleship process with a potential leader, you will learn a few things very quickly about the person interested in serving. Those who are serious about ministering to students will love that there is a clear discipleship plan in place. The process will also filter out those people who were looking for an event-driven ministry. Some potential leaders may show up with a list of "great ideas" that were "awesome" somewhere else. Unfortunately, this person will also share with you why you should do them here and now.

Your loving yet firm response affirming a commitment to the process will prevent the nightmare of misdirected energy. Don't just create a volunteer profile. Show the person how his role is integral to the success of the student ministry, how his role helps students move through the process. For example, a leader who builds relationships with students at the entry point is making students feel welcome. When students know their social needs are being met, spiritual needs can be discussed.

When recruiting potential leaders, ask yourself the big question: *Will this person commit fully to the simple process?* You would rather know now they will not commit instead of six months from now when their roots are in the student ministry. At that point there will be clutter and confusion. All of this can be avoided by not putting the person in leadership.

Leaders who love students will thrive in a simple environment. A clear discipleship process in place is a great recruiting tool. High-quality volunteers are attracted to environments and teams where there is clear direction. Leaders enjoy the direction and parameters that come from utilizing a discipleship process.

Unite Leaders around the Process

Assuming your student ministry has determined *what* type of student disciple you desire to make, designed a process for *how* discipleship will occur, and placed one essential program for each phase of your process, then the programs that require volunteer leadership are obvious. You should now be more committed to these essential programs, so leverage the creativity, energy, time, and leadership of the volunteers God has assembled around those environments.

Utilize the ministry process as a key tool for unity among the leadership team. Let's be honest. Most of the division among leadership teams in ministry occurs not over issues of theology but over issues of methodology. More student pastors have been grilled for their approach to ministry than for their view on eschatology.

By rallying leaders around the ministry process, you are choosing to create unity where disunity can most often fester. You are creating synergy around the *how* of the student ministry.

Parachurch leaders have practiced the principle of mission alignment for years. They are able to attract volunteers from diverse theological backgrounds and unite them on a mission of ministering to students. They wisely hold up the mission piece of the ministry as the unifying factor; thus, they are able to build strong leadership teams.

Local church student ministries should learn a lesson from parachurch ministries. Of course, theology is important and vital. But people unite best around a mission. Unite leaders around the process of your student ministry.

Place and equip leaders in the environments that are vital to your discipleship process. Instead of allowing crucial volunteer time and energy to be utilized in a multitude of directions, utilize your discipleship process to bring focus.

When the team is assembled and placed, ongoing accountability is required to secure and maintain alignment. Without ongoing accountability and rallying the team together, people naturally drift in a variety of directions.

Offer Accountability

Unfortunately many student ministry leaders fear accountability. In the world of student ministry, accountability isn't always popular. Some leaders love student ministry because of the creative and free environment. They find student ministry much less confining than "big people church." But accountability is not the antithesis of creativity and community.

True accountability shouldn't bring fear. By embracing a simple process, your ministry has placed emphasis on discipling students. Honest evaluation and responsibility should be welcomed. With a process in place, there is a framework for evaluation and discussion.

Inspect what you expect is a wise saying. If the student ministry desires for leaders to invest relationally in students, then inspection must exist. If the student ministry desires groups to live on mission in the community, then inspection related to that expectation is essential.

Accountability is not the same as micromanagement. If capable staff and volunteers are micromanaged, their creativity and ability to lead are destroyed. Leaders will play safe and the ministry will suffer and lose its edge.

The polar opposite of micromanagement is neglect. Neglecting accountability creates an environment that lacks excellence, discipline, and execution. Excellence cannot be measured because there is nothing to measure against.

Many student ministries find themselves closer to the neglect side of the scale. Neglect is evident when programs are thrown together, leaders are haphazardly placed in roles, and there is little sense of expectation for God to do something great.

Wise leaders live with the tension between nurturing excellence through accountability and allowing people to lead independently.

The right tools for accountability can maintain alignment. Here are a few tools that will develop accountability in your ministry.

Ministry Action Plan

The Ministry Action Plan (MAP) is an excellent tool for both goal setting and accountability. Eric implemented the MAP at Christ Fellowship, Miami, with all of the staff. Jeff, as a member of Eric's staff, enjoys the process of accountability.

At the beginning of the year, a special time is set aside to develop the MAP. Much time is spent praying and discerning what the next year will look like in terms of ministering to students.

A MAP shows how the ministry reflects the vision and process of the church, how programs are designed to move students through the process, the organizational structure of the ministry, and a present evaluation of the ministry.

Based on the information included in the MAP, five to seven measurable goals are set for the upcoming year and explanation is given as to how those will be accomplished.

The MAP is intended to create goals that work within the framework of the process. The goals are congruous with the process. So literally, the work done every day accomplishes the goals and builds into the discipleship process. "Completing your goals" and then doing "work stuff" are one and the same.

The MAP gives accountability that liberates me (Jeff) to do the work I've been called to do. When fulfilling the goals, the relationships that are necessary to student ministry are being built, and continued emphasis is placed on students growing spiritually.

When all the staff members have completed their MAPs by a scheduled date, they share their MAP, at a staff meeting. Each knows what the others are doing, and they can encourage each other throughout the year.

At various times throughout the year, all staff members again present their MAPs and update each other on how the goals are progressing.

The only time accountability would be awkward or weird would be if Jeff blew off his goals completely. In that case, he would be asking you if you knew anybody that had an opening for a student pastor.

Ask Volunteers for Commitment

Dedicated volunteers make a ministry great. These people are the front line for relationships with students. In effect, many of these people are the "youth pastor" to the students you may never get to build a relationship with.

There is a misconception that you can't hold volunteers accountable because they don't receive a paycheck. However, volunteers committed to a ministry aren't threatened by accountability. They crave it.

Paid staff positions always have an application process, and there should also be an application process for the volunteers in your ministry. In the application packet, put a list of things you expect the leader to do while volunteering in the student ministry. Suggested expectations are:

- Continue to grow in their walk with Christ personally, attend church regularly, and have accountability for their spiritual walk.
- Live a godly life, above reproach as a model to students.
- Be punctual to their committed time or program.
- Attend leader trainings as offered.
- Serve faithfully for one school year.

If there is no standard by which to measure, then accountability will never happen. Nor will excellence. Accountability creates a standard that everyone can live by. Implementing the process everywhere ensures all the ministries within the student ministry are aligned around the same process.

Implement the Process Everywhere

Two guys began a computer company in a garage in 1976. Ten years later, that same company was worth more than two billion dollars and employed four thousand people. Today Apple Inc. has 174 stores around the world, each attracting nearly fourteen thousand visitors per week. (Except for the Fifth Avenue store in New York City, which averages fifty thousand per week!)[3]

If you are fortunate to visit a few of these stores, you will notice a common theme. Though the exterior differs slightly from store to store, the interior consists of stainless steel, polished wood, and glass. The arrangement of the store is mathematical; only 25 percent of the floor is product; the rest of the store is divided by interest: videos, children's interaction, and the Genius Bar (help desk).

One thing missing from every store is clutter. Apple builds and sells fewer than twenty products, so the need for display area and inventory area is reduced. Newer stores have even removed the checkout counter; purchasing your computer can be done with a hand held-device and a credit card.

As Apple grows, the same systems are utilized at each store. You can expect the same great service and product. And the Genius Bar is always present to help you with technical difficulties. The locations not only look very similar but also have the same commitment to remove clutter, offer great service, and sell a superior product in the same fashion.

Student ministries must also be passionate about alignment when growing and replicating programs or ministries. Replication involves great attention to detail. A dedication to your student ministry "DNA" (your process) will ensure full alignment when reproducing.

Overseeing Multiple Ministries

If your student ministry is "fortunate" enough to oversee multiple ministries such as college, teenagers, and children, implement the same simple process in all.

Although the ages of students vary, the desire God has given you to produce spiritually maturing students does not change. The process can be applied to each age demographic but will be contextual in terms of the programming. Programs may look and feel slightly different as students age, but the purpose for the program remains the same.

Overseeing Multiple Campuses

The advent of the multisite church has changed the way some churches manage growth. Instead of building bigger buildings, many churches are choosing to reproduce themselves on another campus in another area of the city or the county.

If your church is presently or will be a multicampus church, implement the simple process on each campus. Imagine the confusion of different campus student ministries having different processes and goals . . . yet being part of the same church!

Although the process will be the same, each program may look different because programming must be contextual. The setup in a theater will be different than the setup in a school cafeteria. A student ministry in farm country will not use the same tools as a student ministry in a downtown area. At the very least, the music will be different.

Community Christian Church in Chicagoland, Illinois, has nine campuses. All of the nine campuses have a student ministry, and all share the same process as the original campus. Their process is: *Celebrate. Connect. Contribute.*

Shawn Williams, student ministry director, oversees the student ministry on each campus and leads one of the student ministries on a campus. According to Shawn, managing campuses without a process in place would be "impossible."

Can you imagine nine different vision statements, various programs, and each still trying to figure out how to produce students who will impact the world? Crazy. And complicated.

Organizationally implementing the process everywhere brings each of the campuses into alignment around the process. Unity is promoted, not because everyone meets in the same room, but because everyone is moving through the same process.

Implement the Process in Your Budget

Your budget should also reflect your discipleship process. Regardless if you receive a budget or if you must bake sale all year to raise funds, how you spend money is a barometer of your priorities. Carefully consider where your money is being spent and the return you are getting for each expenditure.

But if you still do bake sales, please reread the first few chapters of the book.

If your supervisor allows, divide your budget according to your process. If your process is *Connect, Grow, Serve,* then budget money for each program represented in the process. Of course, there will be the extra categories like equipment, training, etc.

Your discipleship process will bring clarity to your budget. You will probably find that you have spent money on less than productive events and programs. Cancel those line items and funnel the money toward the essential aspects of your process.

The truth that your student ministry budget consists of other people's financial giving is humbling. Every dime you spend came from someone's faithfulness to God. As a steward of that money, you must have a clear conscience as to how that money is being spent. Money used must reflect an intentional decision to further discipleship according to the process God has given your student ministry.

Continually Align

Alignment is not a one-time decision. Alignment must continually occur. Just as the tires on your vehicle need ongoing alignment, so does your student ministry.

Just as you will drift from your place on the beach when in the water, ministry will drift unless ongoing alignment takes place. Sometimes you must exit the water and walk down to your spot on the beach before reentering the ocean. Regularly you must evaluate the unity factor in the student ministry and ensure alignment is strong.

New opportunities must be aligned to the overall vision of the student ministry. Before a new facet of the student ministry launches, help the leaders and the students understand how it fits into the whole picture.

For example, if your student ministry launches a drama team because someone saw the "sin box" skit on Godtube or at camp, be sure the leaders and students understand how the drama team fits into the big picture of the student ministry. *Does the drama team help make the entry-level environment more engaging to students? Or can the team be aligned to the mission piece in the student ministry and perform in the community?*

Regardless of where you place new initiatives, ensure they are aligned closely to the process in your student ministry. And please, if you do a drama team, be sure it's good. There's nothing worse than cheesy drama.

Lives Are on the Line

The Coast Guard saved many lives in the days following Hurricane Katrina. Every rescuer knew what was at stake. Every swimmer, pilot, fuel guy, and mechanic was united around the mission of saving lives.

The Coast Guard realized that time was an issue. Every wasted moment equaled a life that could be lost. Lack of direction and disunity would have proved deadly for thousands of people.

Every student ministry can learn much from this example. Every day that our ministries choose to live in disunity, the unbelieving world is affected. People will die today and spend eternity apart from Christ because we refuse to be unified.

A unified student ministry can save lives.

Unity is not uniformity. Uniformity is a means of aligning people to appear as one externally. Unity is deeper. Unity is a matter of the heart. Unity requires laying aside differences that do not matter to achieve a common goal.

Paul prayed that Christians would enjoy unity from God and stand together as one.

> May the God who gives endurance and encouragement give you a spirit of unity among yourselves as you follow Christ Jesus, so that with one heart and mouth you may glorify the God and Father of our Lord Jesus Christ. (Rom. 15:5–6 NIV)

If we were to pray this for our student ministry, it would sound something like this: *Together we follow Christ. Together we lay our preferences aside to pursue what matters in eternity. Together we pursue the vision that God has given us for reaching students.*

A team willing to set aside personal preferences can be a radical force in making student disciples. When we allow the clutter to be removed from the path God has called us to, the real work can begin.

Simple student ministry leaders know the process can unite their team. When most student ministries are divided by complexity, a simple process draws attention and energy to one focus. Being simple is liberating. And it's unifying.

DISCUSSION QUESTIONS

1. Is our ministry unified? Can we honestly say we are aligned around the same vision?
2. What is our current method of recruiting? What do we look for?
3. What kind of accountability do we offer to volunteers?
4. How would a simple process affect the expectations we place on leaders?
5. Do we find it easier to start a new ministry or to stop an existing ministry? Why?
6. How could our approach to alignment be better than it is now?

CHAPTER SIX

Focus

By stripping down an image to its essential meaning,
an artist can amplify that meaning.

—Scott McCloud

O n September 1, 1983, Korean Airlines Flight 007 departed JFK International Airport in New York City. Bound for Seoul, South Korea, the flight carried 269 people, including a U.S. congressman.

Shortly after refueling in Alaska, the plane began to deviate slightly off course. An hour and a half into the flight, the plane was twelve miles off course. Four hours into the flight, KAL 007 was 185 miles north of its flight route.

Though it experienced only a slight change of direction, before long the plane was entering dangerous territory, the Soviet Union. Shortly after KAL 007 entered Soviet airspace for the second time, two Soviet Sukhoi Su-15 fighters near Sakhalin Island, USSR, were ordered to fire two air-to-air missiles. After the missiles hit their target, the plane plummeted into the Sea of Japan. Everyone on board was killed.

What went wrong?

Some argue that the pilots, who were flying via auto-pilot, didn't realize the digression in course until too late. Magnetic positioning used at the time wasn't as reliable or accurate as the current positioning systems. Experts suggest that the navigation crew neglected proper procedures to keep the aircraft on its assigned course.[1]

Regardless, the slight variation in the flight path led to tragedy. Although the deviation was not immediately noticeable, the result was catastrophic. People lost their lives, and families were fundamentally changed because the plane wandered off course.

Staying on Course

Deviation happens every week in student ministry. No ministry plans to deviate from discipleship, but deviation happens and usually with the absolute best of intentions. Many good things can pull a student ministry off course. The philosophy that "more is better" results in a crowded calendar of events and programs. Thus, so much time is spent planning and executing the full calendar that discipleship becomes secondary. The buffet of activities becomes the focus of the student ministry. Deviation can be a killer, even in the smallest of increments.

If you have followed the flow of *Simple Student Ministry* so far, you have defined a discipleship process. And you placed essential programs or environments along your process to effectively move students.

Do you really believe those programs are the best environments to place students? Do you really sense that those are the best environments for life change?

If so, don't you desire all the energy and resources of your student ministry to go toward what your student ministry has declared is essential?

Extra programming, activities, and events will actually get in the way of students moving through the discipleship process. A myriad of programs will steal energy and attention from what your ministry has designed as essential. A cluttered student ministry calendar becomes the enemy of your simple process.

Clutter Divides

Student ministry leaders are often frustrated *when students don't have time for God but have time for everything else.* Granted, ministry can be frustrating when a student ditches something your ministry offers to ride the bench for his water polo team. But if students are asked to attend programs outside your ministry process, their time and energy are split. They may likely attend a nonessential program instead of the few environments your ministry really believes are essential.

Students and their families are extremely busy. Since ministry leaders have only so much of a student's time, that time should be stewarded very wisely. The amount of time students and families give us should be utilized in the environments that we believe are the most conducive for life change.

Some huge questions for a student ministry team to wrestle with are: *How much time do the students in our context have to attend our programs? Is our process and programming reasonable for students to move through?*

Clutter also divides the energy of leaders. Your volunteers are the backbone of your ministry. You will not be able to engage your leaders in significant ministry if they are stretched in multiple places. Every program and event draw from the volunteer's limited pool of energy and time. Calendars must be placed on the microscope of the question, *Am I being a good steward of my volunteer leaders' time?*

Clutter not only divides the energy of leaders and students, but it also divides the limited amount of programming energy. Ministry should be done with quality and excellence. Haphazard ministry is offensive to the nature and character of God. Half-baked messages, cheesy programs, and recycled devotional thoughts thrown together at the last minute are a poor reflection on the excellent God we serve. When a ministry juggles a ridiculous number of programs and events, there is no way each one can be offered with excellence. The energy and resources are spread too thin across the myriad of programs.

The implications of a busy calendar in the lives of your students, leaders, and programming are clear, but what about the effects on your life? Does your busy schedule make you feel as though you have given your best energy for the kingdom, or have you merely been busy?

We've been given twenty-four hours in a day. No more, no less. How is your day best spent? Perhaps you are like many leaders we've met—feeling as though you're accomplishing nothing despite tons of hours of work.

Briefly construct a pie chart of how you spend your time. For the sake of the example, use these three areas: developing yourself (Bible study, reading, etc.), developing others (investing in leaders and students), and developing plans for events or activities.

For the average workweek, what would your pie chart look like? On an annual scale, what would the pie look like? This can be a good indication of where your ministry places its emphasis.

1. Draw the appropriate "slice of pie" that represents the amount of time you spend weekly developing yourself (Bible study, reading, praying, etc.).
2. Next, draw the slice that represents your investment in others (training, discipleship, etc.).
3. Last, draw the slice that represents your investment in your calendar (planning and executing various events and programs outside your discipleship process).

God never ordained the busyness of ministry to be our mistress. However, much of what makes up the overfilled calendar isn't work for eternity. It is fluff for right now.

The Great Deviation

An overprogrammed calendar is also a deviation from discipleship because the calendar keeps students from engaging people who are not yet Christian. And part of discipleship is living among people who are far from God (1 Pet. 2:11–12). The overbooked calendar keeps students in a religious bubble or doing religious stuff and trains them to be Christians away from the world.

We must give students the opportunity to be what Jesus intended for all who follow Him:

> "You are the light of the world. A city situated on a hill cannot be hidden. No one lights a lamp and puts it under a basket, but rather on a lampstand, and it gives light for all who are in the house. In the same way, let your light shine before men, so that they may see your good works and give glory to your Father in heaven." (Matt. 5:14–16)

There is a dichotomy if we tell students to be influences for Christ, yet overload them with religious programs. What does the overprogramming teach students? Perhaps the lesson being learned is to live life in a Christian bubble and fear nonbelievers, or—even worse—consider those away from Christ as the enemy.

Being afraid of lost people or considering them the enemy isn't being a city on a hill but rather hiding the light we were given. Hiding our faith in religious community is easy. Life is comfortable inside the church walls where we need to worry only about what other Christians think.

Jesus didn't take this approach. He lived His life in relation to lost people. In fact, Jesus was accused of being a *friend of sinners*.

In Luke 15, the Pharisees criticized Jesus because He was surrounded by those considered to be the "gangsters" of society at the time, the tax collectors and sinners. Jesus began to share with the Pharisees three short stories about things that were lost: the lost sheep, the lost coin, and the lost son.

Lost people are a priority to God.

If we are followers of Christ, sharing Jesus with lost people should be our priority. How our calendar is planned speaks volumes to this truth. What we choose to focus on in student ministry will speak much louder than what we say is important.

There is a deep relationship between being simple and being missional. Staying on course with your simple process for discipleship will nudge students to missional living and burst the religious bubble created by complex programming.

Do your students see themselves as God's missional agents or members of a youth group? Are your students more attracted to being at another program or watching their friends begin a relationship with Jesus? Whenever we allow our focus to be on anything other than making disciples, we deviate off course. Big time.

We must be willing to say no to even the best ideas that are outside our discipleship process. We must not deviate from the course God has given our ministries. To bring greater focus to your student ministry, eliminate the nonessential, limit adding programs, and reduce special events.

Eliminate the Nonessential

Moses understood focus.

God told Moses to lead the Israelites into the desert to worship. First, leaving Egypt was a necessity. However, Pharaoh was less than excited about the idea. He tried to get Moses to compromise several times.

Exodus chapters 5 to 12 tell the story of Pharaoh's best attempts to get Moses to lose focus. God commanded that all of Israel would leave Egypt: men, women, children, and animals. The entire nation was to go; no one was to be left behind.

Pharaoh threw up some good compromises. *OK. You can worship your God, but stay here in Egypt.*

No.

OK. Only the men go to worship. Then come back.

No.

Pharaoh's offer didn't seem that unreasonable. The Israelites could still have worshipped but would remain in Egypt. Pharaoh made more attempts to convince Moses to compromise, but Moses's answer was still an unwavering no. Leaving Egypt was essential for Israel to be free from bondage.

Everyone had to leave. No other option was available. There would be no deviation.

Say No

Promises. Promises.

You have probably seen the mailers that guarantee if you participate in a particular conference or event, you will be the best-liked, most successful student ministry leader on the planet. There are concerts, festivals, day trips, weekenders, conferences, youth rallies, and the list grows daily.

Other ministries host training programs for that pivotal first year out of high school. *Send your students to us and we'll teach them how to defend their faith and show them how to live the Christian life.*

The truth is, if student ministries were doing the work of discipleship, most of these companies would be out of business.

Let's get real for a moment. What is so fundamentally messed up in student ministry that we have to send our students away to be taught how to live as "sold out" Christians? How did we lose our focus? Where did the deviation begin?

A program-cluttered calendar sends a very clear message: *We aren't able to teach you what you need to know, so you will have to go somewhere else.* The result is students are inadvertently trained to look for the next big thing to *really* learn about God and experience Him firsthand.

When you remove everything outside your process, your focus is on the essential programs that place students in the path of discipleship.

An Example from Jeff's Ministry

In the spring of 2006, the student ministry of Christ Fellowship, Miami, evaluated the necessity of summer camp in light of its discipleship process. After returning from a mission trip to help rebuild Bay St. Louis, Mississippi, from Hurricane Katrina, the leaders discussed the spiritual fruit from mission trips in comparison to the spiritual fruit from summer camp.

The leadership began to ask some hard questions. *Where does summer camp fit into our discipleship process? What type of spiritual fruit do we see from summer camp? How does summer camp help us move people through the process? Does the fruit from camp remain?*

The fruits from summer camp were some salvations, a lot of excitement, new friendships, and a lot of fun memories. Those things were all awesome.

Even though some students made decisions for Christ, the massive budget and countless hours of planning led the team to the conclusion that if the camp were only about evangelism, there had to be a better way. Making a kid pay $300 dollars to tell him about Jesus didn't seem right. And more students were engaged in the weekly entry-level program than were engaged in summer camp.

The fruits from mission trips were people on the mission field getting saved, students becoming unified, lessons learned in serving others, and spiritual growth that lasted more than a couple of weeks after the trip. The momentum from mission trips was actually carrying over when students went to school. Students were impacting their friends for Christ because they experienced sharing their faith on a trip.

The decision to eliminate was made. Summer camp was kicked to the curb like an overeager prom date. The week usually reserved for wakeboarding or going out west was replaced with another mission trip.

The decision wasn't popular in the beginning. A few students and some parents voiced their opposition. But now there are more students engaging in missions than were ever engaged in a camp experience. And the weekly programming is more resourced and supported with the line items that used to finance camp.

After the first summer mission trip, the subject of summer camp was never mentioned again. Now, *When are we going back?* to the place of our last mission trip is asked often. In fact, when a mission trip is announced, cheers usually follow.

Some hard questions must be asked in student ministry. *Is everything that we do worth the investment?* If not, we must begin to cut. Trim the fat. Call Jenny Craig; there are some things to lose, but much more to gain.

What if the money spent on a nonessential program or event was reinvested into the programs that move students through your discipleship process? How different would the programs look? If all the events and extra programs aren't working, allocate that money for use in your existing programs and do them with greater excellence.

Limit Adding Programs

When Southwest Airlines began, its vision was simple: be *the* low-cost airline. Everything in the company is aligned around that simple goal. But to remain simple, Southwest has a disciplined approach toward new ideas and opportunities.

One day a high-level employee presented an idea to the former CEO, Herb Kelleher. The employee attempted to convince Kelleher that customers would be happier if a small meal was provided on long flights. Perhaps a chicken salad sandwich. Something small.

Kelleher asked if the chicken salad sandwich would help make Southwest *the* low-cost airline. Obviously the answer was no; therefore, no sandwich was added.[2]

Adding programs to your existing process can prevent your ministry from realizing the vision God has given you. Even a well-intentioned addition can cause deviation.

Although the programs placed along your process will look different over the years, you must fight to keep simple. So what do you do when a specific emphasis is needed in your student ministry?

Funnel the content through an existing program instead of beginning something new. Since adding another program only causes complexity, use existing programs.

Assume a leader is ready to teach guys about the importance of purity of mind and body. Lust is a difficult topic for many guys, and the truth needs to be told. The teaching can be funneled into an essential program in your process, such as small groups or an equivalent. Simply use existing programming and choose purity as the topic.

Offer more options, not more programs.

There is a huge difference between adding options and adding programs. Offering the same program multiple times is simply offering more options. And options are a great thing because students are given more opportunities to attend the essential programs in your process.

For example, a student ministry that offers more than one small-group opportunity for students is simply offering more options for a student to plug into a group. It is another program if the purpose and structure of each group is different, and if the student is asked to attend multiple groups.

If groups are only offered one place and one time during the week, students who can't make that time frame are alienated and out of luck. Offering groups at different times throughout the week isn't adding another program; more options are given to attend one program.

If your student area during any program is 80 percent full, another option for the same program will lift the lid for growth. In this case, simple ministry leaders understand that adding another service immediately before or after the existing service is adding another option. This is not a whole new program, rather the exact same service offered another time for the sake of space and convenience for those who come.

Multisite churches understand this concept. When a church starts another campus, everything offered at the original campus is extended to a different location and different times. The option is awesome for those who do not live close to the original campus. The other campus option is also a great way to reach a different area of the city.

The strategy of *options not programs* makes reproducing a ministry much easier. A simple process and programming philosophy is essential in reproduction. Simple is always more reproducible than complex.

Reduce Special Events

Kyle MacDonald was renting an apartment, but he really wanted to own a house. The writer/trade show representative, who didn't have a lot of money, came up with a creative idea to own a house. He used a game called "bigger and better" to pursue home ownership.

His journey began with one red paper clip.

Kyle began by posting his proposition to trade up his red paper clip on Craigslist, an online classified ads service. One year after posting his paper clip on the Internet, he owned a home in Canada.[3]

Amazingly Kyle did not spend one penny of his own money to make the trades. Some of his biggest trades included a snowmobile, a moving truck, a day hanging out with Alice Cooper, and a KISS snow globe. The snow globe was traded to actor Corbin Bernsen for the small acting job that set him up for the house.

Trading a house for a single red paper clip did not happen on accident; the pursuit was intentional and took relentless initiative. Kyle focused solely on items that increased his chance of getting a house.

One amazing detail of the story is that there were only fourteen trades. A paper clip. Fourteen trades. A house. The difference in value between a paper clip and a house is so vast that logically more trades would have been necessary.

But Kyle wasn't merely hoping to get a house; he traded with focus and intention, only trading up to something that would lead him closer to his ultimate goal of owning a home. Kyle didn't make trades just to keep trading. Each trade had to lead closer to his goal—closer to a home.

By keeping his number of trades at fourteen, Kyle invested thought and time into each trade. Without focus, he potentially could have made some bad trades and slowed the process. Less productive trades would have been a deviation.

In the same way, the longer your process is the less likely students will be able to move through it. The more programming, the less likely they will be able to attend what your student ministry believes is most essential. And the more events surrounding your process, the less attention your essential programs receive.

Everything your ministry offers must intentionally lead students toward spiritual maturity. In order to focus on the discipleship process for your students, you must limit the number of special events. Events require time, energy, and commitment that ultimately distract from your process.

We aren't saying special events aren't fun. We aren't saying that nothing good comes from special events. We are simply saying that events can be a distraction, a deviation from your discipleship process.

Fully committing to your discipleship process requires time and investment. Unlike events, the development of the essential programs in your student ministry process is not a one-time investment. When time is invested in the steps that facilitate movement, the results are ongoing. Energy that would be spent planning extra activities is poured into what is essential. Programs are creatively developed. Steps between programs are simplified. Leaders are trained. None of this is possible when there is the constant pressure to perform and produce the next big event.

So what does a simple student ministry do with all the events? Other than simply eliminating them, here are some practical suggestions.

Tag the event with an existing program.

Combine the special event with one of your essential programs. By doing so, additional energy will be placed on an essential program, and new students will experience something your ministry offers every week.

Some simple student ministries offer activities before and after their student ministry services on a weekly basis. Basketball, skateboarding, and dodge ball are all great games, but instead of offering these separate from the weekly gathering, tag them to your weekly gathering. Leaders are placing these fun activities either right before or after their entry-point service.

Events such as a holiday party, movie nights, a burger-eating competition, or a great game of ultimate Frisbee can be attached to an existing program. You can kill two birds with one stone by attaching special events to an entry-point program. Students who normally come will enjoy the event, but this also provides a great incentive to invite their friends. The guests will have a blast and get the opportunity to experience a weekly program and meet people in your ministry.

This principle not only works well for events with students, but for many other aspects of ministry. For example, when a leader needs to meet with small-group leaders and discuss upcoming curriculum, the training can be tagged to the already scheduled small-group night. If many of the leaders meet on one night, near or in the same place, having the leaders' meeting before or after their small group simplifies the calendar.

Consider offering your parent meetings immediately before or after one of the programs in the process. Plan the parent meeting when the parents will already be around. Parents can come earlier or stay later rather than committing hours a different day out of an already busy week.

Be sure there is a clear next step.

If you offer an event that is not combined with one of your essential programs, be sure there is a clear next step for those who attend the event. You can determine the next step by asking, *What do we want the students to do after the event?*

Think on-ramp, not cul-de-sac.

When offering an event, view the event as an on-ramp to an essential program in your process. Otherwise, the event is a cul-de-sac and results in no forward movement. If you offer a Disciple Now weekend or a fall retreat, consider using your weekly group leaders as the hosts (instead of people from another state), so that the event helps build deeper community in current groups and moves new students to groups. If you desire to promote missions in public schools and plan on offering a training session outside your weekly programming, be sure the event strategically matches students together so that there is a next step for them on their campus.

Most organizations ministering to students specialize in big events. Most events are designed around a "reach out" philosophy or some type of "fellowship." Truthfully, most student ministries have perfected fellowship.

There must be more depth to our programming.

Discipleship must be the new focus.

You must pursue only events that help nudge students through your process. Great care must be taken to ensure that any event is tagged to your process or helps directly move students into some aspect of your discipleship process.

Forceful Focus

If you have truly designed a discipleship process that your ministry believes in, point all the energy and resources to the process God has given you. For your student ministry to be great, a forceful focus to what God has called you to do is essential.

John the Baptist understood the focus required with being great.

John the Baptist was called John the Baptist because he baptized people. His name was descriptive of what he did, not because he was a part of the Baptist denomination. Some Baptists would not have liked John. He did not eat that much. He would have showed up empty-handed at a potluck supper or dinner party. His diet was locusts and honey.

John was a prophet who preached repentance of sins to Israel. The people of Israel had not heard a word of the Lord from a prophet in four hundred years. The people were desperate for some word from God, fearing that He had abandoned them or forgotten them.

John the Baptist came dressed like a prophet from way back. He reminded people of Elijah and his message was similar to Elijah's. He wore a robe of camel's hair and a leather belt around his waist (see Matt. 3:4). People came from miles throughout the entire region to hear the new Elijah—to hear John the Baptist's message of repentance (sec Matt. 3:1–5). John the Baptist created great expectation throughout all of Israel. He was predicating a new day, as the Messiah was coming. John was constantly pointing people to Jesus the Messiah.

John was Jesus' cousin, born approximately six months before Christ. John the Baptist's mother was Elizabeth, who was a cousin to Mary, Jesus' mother. His father was Zechariah. Zechariah was a priest of God, and one day the angel Gabriel came to Zechariah while he was performing some of his priestly responsibilities and told him that he would have a son.

The angel told Zechariah that his son would be great in the sight of the Lord (Luke 1:15) and that he would bring many people back to God (Luke 1:16). Zechariah couldn't believe it. He was old in age so he said, "But I am an old man, how can I be sure of this?" Gabriel silenced Zechariah's mouth and told him he would not speak until the child was born because he doubted, which was surely a relief to his wife during her pregnancy.

Six months later, the same angel Gabriel, approached Mary and told her that she would give birth to the Christ (see Luke 1:32). The angel also told Mary that her cousin Elizabeth was pregnant in her old age even though she was said to be barren. Mary was so excited to be the one chosen to give birth to the Messiah, but she was also excited to be pregnant. She hurried to visit Elizabeth so they could celebrate together (see Luke 1:39–40) and perhaps register at the local Babies "R" Us. Pregnant women have always enjoyed being together.

When Mary entered Elizabeth's house, the baby in Elizabeth's womb leaped for joy. When John first met Jesus, even in the womb, he was thrilled. John the Baptist was always excited to be in the presence of Christ.

When John was born, his father was able to speak again and he prophesied about his son: that he would prepare the way for the Lord, that he would give people the knowledge of salvation (see Luke 1:76–77). And *Jesus* literally means salvation.

John effectively fulfilled his life mission of preparing people for Christ. John's one life was great. Jesus spoke of John's greatness:

> I tell you the truth: Among those born of women there has not risen anyone greater than John the Baptist; yet he who is least in the kingdom of heaven is greater than he. From the days of John the Baptist until now, the kingdom of heaven has been forcefully advancing, and forceful men lay hold of it. (Matt. 11:11–12 NIV)

Wow. Jesus said that there had yet to be anyone as great as John. No one had yet stepped up like John. No one had yet risen to the level of greatness as John the Baptist.

And one of the reasons his life was great was because he was *forceful* for the kingdom of God. Jesus bragged on John the Baptist because after John showed up on the scene, the kingdom of God expanded rapidly.

Forceful is not something we typically associate with the Christian message or the Christian faith. We often think that to be a good Christian means to be the antithesis of forceful and aggressive; instead, be mild, timid, soft-spoken, and basically a doormat for the world to trample on. We have domesticated the wild and forceful nature of our faith, making it safe, tame, and sometimes even boring. Thus the faith is seldom thought about in terms of being forceful and radical.

Yet Jesus said that John the Baptist's life was greater than all. And he was forceful and focused. He sought only to point people to the coming Christ, to prepare the way for the Lord (see Matt. 3:11). He refused to let people associate him with the Messiah (see Luke 3:16). His pilgrimage to the desert as a young man prepared him for his life mission (see Luke 1:80). His fascination with Christ, even from the womb (see Luke 1:44), drove him to press forward in his walk with God.

John was passionately focused on expanding the kingdom of God. He fulfilled the birth announcement that the angel Gabriel gave Zechariah about John: "Many of the people of Israel will he bring back to the Lord their God" (Luke 1:16 NIV).

You have been invited to be a part of God's mission of expanding His kingdom through ministry to students. It is the greatest cause to join, the best battle to be in, and the greatest fight of your life. And the kingdom of God is not for the faint at heart. *Forceful men lay hold of it.* The mission requires our deep commitment because the stakes are so high. People's eternal destiny hangs in the balance. The mission requires forceful focus.

As David Putman, one of the pastors of Mountain Lake Church in Cumming, Georgia, told Eric in a conversation about staying focused on your simple process: "We are mean about our vision."

Without a forceful focus, ministry will drift toward complexity. Drifting toward disorder is actually a law of nature, meaning it really does happen. Drift will take place unless we are mean about the vision God has given us. Drift will occur unless we correct the slight deviations in our ministries.

What happened the night of September 1, 1983? We may never know why the flight drifted into Soviet airspace. We know for sure only that flight KAL 007 was off course and that deviation was the reason for its tragic ending. Despite the plane being off course, the direction of the plane could have been corrected and brought back into focus. The flight would have landed in Korea. Lives would have been saved, and families would still be together.

God has placed you in leadership. If your ministry has overemphasized programs and neglected real discipleship, pull the ministry back into focus. It's time to be mean with the vision for student ministry God has given you.

DISCUSSION QUESTIONS

1. If we were starting our student ministry from scratch, are there any weekly programs we would consider not offering?
2. Does our current programming help move students to a point of mission? How can we improve on this?
3. Are there any special events we should consider not offering or tagging to essential programs?
4. For those events we do, what is the clear next step?
5. If we had 20 percent more volunteer time and financial resources, where would we place that energy? Can we gain the extra time and resources by eliminating something(s)?
6. What would *forceful with our mission* look like in our context?

CHAPTER SEVEN

Large and Megachurch Case Studies

Christianity means a lot more
than church membership.

—Billy Sunday

L arge churches and large ministries are often extremely complex and complicated. Typically the church enjoyed a simple philosophy and entrepreneurial spirit during its formative years of growth. But with the additional ideas and resources, complex levels of programming crept in. And now, enormous amounts of energy and resources are expended to maintain the system.

Many large churches and ministries admit they have reached a sustained period of stagnancy. They also admit that they long to be simple, to funnel their resources to a few activities that will make the biggest impact for the kingdom.

Being simple and being large are often very difficult. As a church or ministry grows, it really must fight to stay simple and focused.

We chose the following student ministries as case studies because of their commitment to a discipleship process. We are not saying these student ministries are successful because they are large and have more building space or cooler stuff. We've spoken with many large student ministries that could not clearly articulate how they disciple students.

We are saying, however, these student ministries are successful because they disciple students intentionally. They will do whatever it takes to place students in environments where they can be transformed by the power of God.

Crossroads Community Church, Simpsonville, South Carolina

Crossroads Community Church in South Carolina is home to CRCC Student Ministry. The church attendance averages around eight hundred people per week, including ninety high school students. Dustin Hughes, student pastor, and the staff of Crossroads Community implemented their discipleship process in 2006.

CRCC Student Ministry believes making disciples is accomplished by following its process: *Our goal is to make disciples through encountering God, connecting to others, and serving their world.*

High school students encounter God at a Sunday night worship service called Encounter, connect to others by joining a small group, and serve their world by ministering in the church and performing missions in the world.

The following graph explains the programming at CRCC Students.

Encountering God

Sunday nights are designed for encountering God. This program is based on four elements that students should experience: worship, teaching, testimony, and prayer. CRCC Student Ministry leadership believes these elements are important for teenagers to open their hearts to God.

The youth area opens at 5:30 p.m. for anyone who comes early to pray for the service. Some teenagers show up at 6 p.m. to hang out with friends or just play games and hang out.

At 6:30 p.m. students are welcomed to Encounter, and they join together in prayer. The band leads worship in songs that reflect what the message is about, and encourages students to seek God's face authentically.

A message is shared from the Bible, and time is given for response to what's been heard. As the band finishes its second set, every aspect of the service points to God and the need for an encounter with Him.

CRCC STUDENT MINISTRY

Our goal? Make disciples.

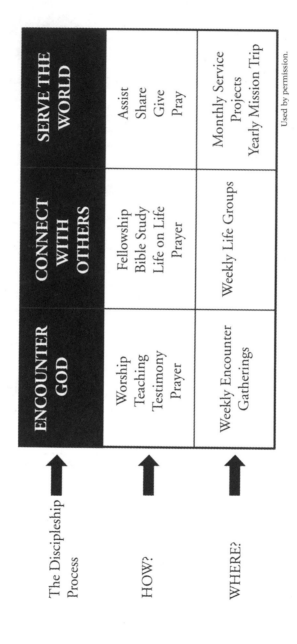

	ENCOUNTER GOD	CONNECT WITH OTHERS	SERVE THE WORLD
The Discipleship Process →	Worship Teaching Testimony Prayer	Fellowship Bible Study Life on Life Prayer	Assist Share Give Pray
HOW? →			
WHERE? →	Weekly Encounter Gatherings	Weekly Life Groups	Monthly Service Projects Yearly Mission Trip

Used by permission.

CRCC Student Ministry knows that growing spiritually won't happen on one's own; students must be connected to others. Each week students are reminded either by announcements or personal invitation to join a Life Group with other students who are moving forward in their relationship with Christ.

Connecting to Others

Life Groups are small groups where high school students do life together. These groups are separated by age and gender and meet in homes throughout the week. Usually a couple of caring adults teach and invest in the lives of students.

While the focus of Life Groups is to learn biblical truth and build solid relationships, groups have the freedom to switch the focus of a night if necessary. Instead of the regular study, the group can focus on accountability or discuss and pray for an issue a group member is experiencing. Flexibility allows groups to meet needs on a more intimate level.

Life Groups also serve the community quarterly. Serving gets the groups out of their comfort zones and ministering together.

For example, an eleventh-grade girl's Life Group went to a shelter for battered women and their children. The girls baked and took cookies for everyone and cared for the children while tired mothers got a chance to relax.

The afternoon concluded with the girls talking with the moms about their situation and praying for the moms and children.

Bible study is very important, but so is the application of all that has been learned. Students must be given opportunities to be the hands and feet of Jesus. The leadership realizes that when students can live out what they have learned, the desire to serve increases.

At the Encounter service and in Life Groups, students are urged to serve their world. In order to make the step to serving clear, opportunities to serve are communicated via flyers, blogs, and announcements from the stage.

Serving Their World

Students get experience serving others in ministries for students and adults. Teenagers can be seen every weekend serving in the children's area or the youth area or helping with adult ministries. High school students who are growing in their faith and showing signs of leadership are invited to join the leadership team. This group serves by leading in middle school small groups each week.

CRCC Student Ministry also helps other less fortunate student ministries in the Simpsonville area by partnering with and serving them. For instance, a leader and some students will show up at another church's youth service with free pizza for everyone and share in the ministry for that evening. After the service is over, the team helps clean up areas of the church.

The student ministry also offers the opportunity to reach out to the community one night per month. One night the ministry accepted food donations and gave them to the local food bank. On another occasion students handed out free bottles of water with the church name on them to make an impression on pedestrians in the downtown area.

Students who get opportunities to live out what they have learned experience transformation. A lightbulb comes on. All the lessons about serving others make sense.

CRCC Student Ministry understands the importance of a discipleship process. A student must encounter God, grow with others, and learn to serve. Placing students in the right environments gives them the greatest opportunity for transformation.

Dustin Hughes, student pastor of CRCC Students, said this about having a plan for discipleship,

> The process is very easy to explain to people.
> Instructing people on what discipleship looks like
> is clearer than anything I have ever experienced . . .
> this also helps our staff know that what we do aligns
> with who we are. We don't feel the pressure to be
> program driven or calendar filling. We don't feel like
> we have to be doing, doing, doing to be successful as
> a ministry.

Christ Fellowship, Miami, Florida

CF Students is the student ministry of Christ Fellowship, a church comprising five campuses across Miami-Dade County. The church attendance averages forty-five hundred people per week, including six hundred students.

Research shows that Miami-Dade is the second most unchurched county in the United States. Interestingly, more than 50 percent of the Miami residents were born outside of the country. With such a diversity of culture and no dominant Christian influence, discipleship must be clear.

Christ Fellowship implemented a simple process in 2004 and has been tweaking programs and removing events ever since. The student ministry shares the same discipleship process as the church: *CF Students exists to connect students to God, to others, to ministry, and to the world.* Christ Fellowship visually illustrates its discipleship process with the following diagram.

CF Students uses a weekend worship service to connect students to God, small groups to connect to others, serving inside the church to connect to ministry, and living on mission to connect to the world.

Connect to God

It's Saturday night and the café area on the second floor is buzzing with the noise of excited friends catching up from the week. Some sophomores have met together to talk and enjoy some iced coffee. A few eighth-graders are

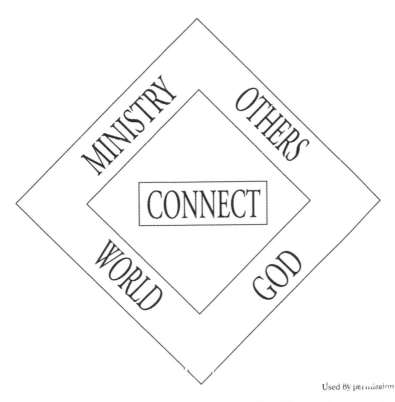

still out at the skate park trying to pull off one last kick flip before the middle school service begins.

Teenagers have stopped their Saturday activities to attend CF Students. Whether they just came from the beach or the basketball court or rode their skateboards to the service, students have come to connect to God.

CF Students designs its worship service knowing that teenagers need to be connected to God. This reality affects every aspect of the worship service programming; every song, every video, and even the icebreaker tie into the truth that will be shared from God's Word. And, prayerfully, lives will be changed for the glory of God.

In the worship service, students sit at tables situated around the room. The tables provide a relational environment, which seats facing forward do not. These tables allow time for discussion and connect guests immediately with students in the ministry.

A competent leader facilitates discussion at the tables and helps guests feel welcome. At the end of the service, leaders counsel students about spiritual issues. Also, table leaders provide guidance for students who aren't really interested in hearing about God but manage to show up anyway.

Take Shephathiah, for example. As a freshman in high school, Sheph showed up to the weekend service dressed in a tie and looking sharp. His heart, however, was completely disconnected from what was happening in the worship service. He and his friends refused to stand during worship and talked during the sermon. He was a punk. The table was full of guys like Sheph. They were in a worship service but completely disconnected.

However, his table leaders, Maria and Geoff, never gave up on him or his buddies. The leaders loved them when other leaders were ready to toss them out of the ministry. And the tableful of guys kept coming back.

After the murder of a close friend, Sheph gave his heart to Jesus and stayed plugged into the student ministry. Sheph began to grow in his faith and share his love for Jesus with his friends.

Now Sheph is an intern for the student ministry, and a few of the friends from that table serve as volunteers. The table leaders who wouldn't stop loving the guys are still serving students today.

Even though the worship services are engaging and great lessons are taught, CF Students believes deeper discipleship must take place in small groups. Developing authentic relationships is difficult in the large-group setting.

In order to encourage movement to a small group, CF Students works to remove any barriers or extra steps that might hinder moving to the next phase of the process. These include unclear information about small-group time and location, misunderstanding of how to join a small group, and ignorance of the purpose of small groups.

Several steps were put into place to remove barriers and improve movement.

First, small-group leaders are encouraged to be table leaders at a worship service. The groups at these tables build relationships naturally; a leader invites the kids to the table to join his or her small group. That's a home run. The personal invitation is the most effective of moving tools.

Second, students share on video during the worship service the importance of small groups in their lives. When a student can authentically share how the small group has impacted him or her, the importance of small groups makes an "aha" moment in the mind of those who are listening.

Last, small groups are promoted in sermons and announcements. The speaker weaves the subject of community and accountability into the context of the message and shares how his personal group has affected his life.

Announcements also voice the importance of community and how to get connected. When an announcement is made or special emphasis is given during a message, a leader is at an information table in the room to answer questions and encourage sign-up. In ideal situations, students are also at the small-group table to meet anyone interested.

CF Students believes that if teenagers attend the weekend worship service and attend small groups, they will connect to God and build healthy relationships.

Connect to Others

Small groups are the second phase of the process. Small groups meet at various times throughout the week in homes, schools, and on the church campus. These groups encourage interaction and open discussion about spiritual issues. In the process of learning and growing in their relationship with Christ, students have accountability and relationships with like-minded friends.

Small-group leaders are godly adults who range in age from nineteen to sixty-three. The curriculum for small groups reflects what is being taught at the worship service, with greater opportunity for discussion.

Small groups are encouraged to "live out the one anothers of the Bible." In this context, the groups study, learn, play, and serve together. Small groups have overnighters and other bonding activities that will not happen at the large-group level. These "one anothers" of the Bible cannot happen in ninety minutes once a week.

Small groups also do "reach beyonds." Christ Fellowship encourages small groups at every age level to serve the community in a tangible way. Reach beyonds get the groups into the community to show the love of Jesus.

For example, a group of ninth-grade boys and their crazy leader, Anthony, went to a local restaurant and cleaned the toilets for free. After taking before and after pictures of their work, the group thanked the manager and gave him a business card that said, "God loves you" with the name and information of Christ Fellowship on the back.

Another small group, composed of junior and senior girls, adopted a local teen pregnancy home. These amazing girls tutored the future moms, gave rides to various places, threw baby showers, and shared the love of Jesus with teenage girls most people would shun. (On a side note, the girls who did the ministering did not follow in the footsteps of the pregnant girls. Just in case someone in your ministry is convinced that will happen.)

Small groups aren't designed to hide away and have *another* Bible study; students apply what they have learned to everyday life and prayerfully move forward in their relationships with God. Everyone who attends small groups is encouraged to move to the next level of discipleship: ministry.

Serving others is vital in growing relationship with Christ so students are pushed (in a good way) to serve somewhere in the church. In a few ways CF Students is making the move from small groups to ministry a little easier:

- When a ministry team has a need, the ministry is highlighted at the worship service. Sign-up is available at the back of the room, and a contact person is available to answer questions. Students can connect immediately and get questions answered.

- Leaders of other ministries are encouraged to build relationships with students and recruit. Instead of the student ministry announcing all the other ministries, the relational approach is more effective.

- Serving is emphasized a few times a year, usually coupled with a video testimony of how serving has impacted a life. Information cards are placed on each table and students can sign up immediately.

Serving allows students to experience what Jesus taught the disciples in Mark 10. The lesson becomes a lifestyle that lasts for a lifetime.

Connect to Ministry

Teenagers can serve on a ministry team in the student area or another area or campus of the church. Many students serve in the preschool ministry, elementary ministry, media team, drama team, worship band, and other places around campus.

First Friends, an example of a great ministry team, is the greeting team that welcomes people at the doors of the worship service but also helps to assimilate guests. Guests are encouraged to fill out a guest card and afterward are escorted by a First Friend through the youth facility. The guest is introduced to other teenagers and to adult leaders, then joins the First Friend at his or her table for the worship service.

Serving others gives ownership of the ministry and teaches the godly discipline of placing the needs of others first. Serving is about more than just filling available spots; the right people are needed in the right places for the ministry to be successful.

Students are challenged to serve in ministry and are also encouraged to reach out to the world on a local, national, and global scale.

Mission opportunities are mentioned in sermons, announced at worship services, and celebrated by video when completed. Applications for trips are available online and after each worship service. The most powerful motivation to do mission work is the personal invitation of a friend.

Connect to the World

In order to connect to the world, students are given opportunities to do local, national, and global missions every year.

First, students are encouraged to "invest and invite" by building relationships with lost friends and inviting them to Christ. If the teenager isn't comfortable leading a friend to Christ yet, then the goal is to invite that person to CF Students where he or she will hear the gospel clearly. Tag-on events to weekend worship services give extra incentives for guests to come check out the ministry. Business card invites are also available to make the invitation clear and concise.

Second, mission trips are offered within the city of Miami, the state of Florida, and other parts of the United States. CF Students has traveled to Tampa, Mississippi, and New Orleans to invest in people and share Jesus.

Third, Christ Fellowship sends teams overseas every year for one to six weeks at a time. Mission trips to South Africa, Cuba, South America, and the Ukraine are all open to teenagers.

CF Students understands focus. As a ministry, it asks their students to do only four things: connect to God, to others, to ministry, and to the world. With multiple services on many campuses, students can sit in a worship service and serve in a ministry in the same day. At some point in the week, they should attend a small group and live missionally.

Community Christian Church, Naperville, Illinois

Student Community is the student ministry of Community Christian Church. Community Christian is a multisite church with nine separate locations; all of which have a student presence. The church averages about fifty-one hundred people per weekend, including five hundred fifty students.

Shawn Williams oversees the student ministry and leads ministry on the largest campus. On his arrival at Community Christian, a discipleship process for the entire church was already in place. Shawn brought the student ministry into greater alignment.

Alignment is also a huge factor with multiple student ministries on different campuses. If each campus were pursuing discipleship different ways, the result would be chaos.

The key words for discipleship at Student Community are: *Celebrate, Connect, and Contribute*. Community Christian views its process as cyclical. Regardless of where students enter the process, they are encouraged to become "3C" Christ followers. Here are the programs or "experiences" that Student Community uses to disciple students.

Celebrate

Picture a room filled with teenagers of all shapes and sizes singing along with the music led by the band on stage.

The lights are low and hands raise energetically in worship as voices sing along to the words on the screen. Each week students gather on Wednesday nights at a creative worship experience with vibrant worship, videos, and a relevant message from God's Word.

Students are challenged to celebrate God in their personal lives by reading the Bible daily and journaling about lessons they have learned.

This is StuCo, the worship service for Student Community.

When students arrive at StuCo, they are divided by middle school and high school. From 7 to 8 p.m. the younger students enjoy the celebration service while high school students enjoy hanging out in the café and playing games. At 8 p.m., the age groups switch places; middle school students hang out and build relationships while high school students enjoy the service.

After being connected to the StuCo celebration service, movement is encouraged to the next phase of discipleship: small groups.

StuCo encourages movement to small groups by highlighting a small group during a service. The entire group may come on stage or the leader of a group might share why small groups are important. The leadership will also give the small-group program special emphasis for a couple weeks at a time in the celebrate service. Occasionally, a mailer is sent out encouraging students to move to small groups.

Emphasizing small groups in the celebration service allows students to see what a small group is like and how to join. Small groups are the second phase of the process and facilitate godly, nurturing relationships.

Connect

Small-group times vary by age and location. The middle school ministry has small groups every weekend on the church campus. High school small groups meet in various homes and places on different nights of the week. Regardless of age, students are regularly encouraged to become part of a small group.

The focus of small groups is to build healthy relationships with other Christians. Students who attend these small groups are in the best possible place to experience true biblical community and grow in their faith. Because small groups are about more than attendance, everyone is encouraged to get into each other's lives and genuinely care for each other's needs.

The celebration service and small groups are tied together by topic. Lessons taught in large-group settings on Wednesday are further discussed in small groups. Questions raised during the teaching can get clarity during discussion. Student Community refers to this as the "Big Idea," a key aspect of the discipleship process.

Small groups also serve together. One of the Community Christian campuses is at a local high school.

A group of high school guys gets up early on Sunday mornings to "unpack" the campus from trailers to prepare for services. When the day is over, the guys pack the equipment back into the trailers and head home.

One of the members of the group commented, "The most rewarding thing about doing this as a small group is you get to see the accomplished effort that our team has put together. We get to see a finished product when we are done working."

Students who attend the celebration service and small groups are encouraged to move further in their relationship with God by serving others. To encourage students to move forward, a specific ministry is highlighted at a celebration service, and students will be encouraged to check it out. Small-group leaders also encourage students in conversation to build a bridge between small groups and serving.

When students engage in serving others, they move to the Contribute phase.

Contribute

Student Community places a high value on contribution. Contributing students realize that God can use them for His glory and that they are instrumental in ministering to others.

Student Community leadership encourages contribution often, with great intensity, challenging students to serve others by joining a ministry team. Students have opportunities to serve each week by being part of the band or media team, serving in a children's program, or being part of the First Impressions team.

It is important to note that plugging into the life of the church isn't designed to keep teenagers busy. The leadership at Student Community believes that if students do not connect with the rest of the church, the ministry will become a silo. When a ministry becomes a silo, it becomes consumed with its own interests and is disconnected from the rest of the church. When this happens, there is no sense of team. A struggle for the ministry's interest to be on top will emerge. The team becomes divided.

Student Community also believes that when students serve in other areas of the church, their involvement will help reduce the risk of leaving the church after graduation. Leadership believes students are a part of the greater body and should serve in other areas of the church.

Contribute is an environment to grow closer to God. The experiences are offered because the goal of Student Community is to produce servant-hearted kids who aren't focused on themselves. Serving is also an experience that opens the door for students to see how they can contribute to the life of the church.

Students are also mobilized for different opportunities to impact their community. Contribution not only happens on campus, but in the community as well. 3C students are in a great place to grow and impact the world.

Shawn summed up his experience with a discipleship process perfectly, "As a leader I have to communicate what God intends for our lives. The simpler the model and more compelling the direction, the better traction we see in the lives of students."

Grace Baptist Church, Cedarville, Ohio

Radiate Student Ministry is the high school ministry of Grace Baptist Church in Cedarville. The church averages about twelve hundred people in attendance during the college school year, including sixty-five students in the high school ministry.

In August 2005 the leadership at Grace Baptist implemented a new discipleship process, and the high school ministry was given the name Radiate. After much prayer and discussion, the high school ministry implemented the *G3 Philosophy of Ministry: Gospel, Grow, and Go.*

Students connect to the gospel at a worship service, grow by attending Bible study, and go by serving others. The following graphic is how the ministry visually represents its process.

Gospel

On a Wednesday night in a town surrounded by cornfields, there isn't much going on. Unless, of course, you are at the high school worship service of Grace Baptist Church. Radiate is a high-energy, student-friendly service

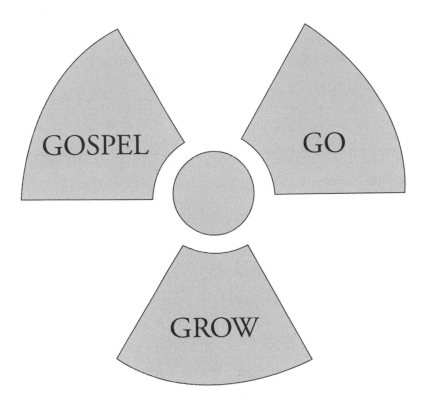

that facilitates the opportunity to build relationships and have a good time.

The service isn't only about the music and the fun, although there is plenty of each. The purpose of Wednesday night is to teach practical Bible lessons that can be applied to life. The leaders at Radiate aren't satisfied with students only showing up for a service; they want to see lives transformed by God.

Toward the end of the Radiate service, students break into small groups to answer questions about the night's message. If a student needs to make a spiritual decision, a leader follows up with him or her during this time. Guests are encouraged to be part of these smaller groups as a way to meet people and assimilate into the ministry.

Leaders go one step further to disciple students by going out to eat with them and spending time together apart from the regularly scheduled group time.

While in these groups, leaders invite students to move to Sunday morning study, the *next* aspect of the process.

Grow

A deeper, more intense Bible study is held on Sunday mornings and represents the *Grow* phase of the process.

The Sunday morning study is held at the church's regular Sunday school time. Students gather for this service in the youth area and learn topics and truths with deeper content than are taught on Wednesday night. Fewer students attend on Sunday morning than on Wednesday night because of the nature of programming. The Sunday teaching requires a greater level of commitment to attend.

Students who are involved with the *Grow* aspect of the process are encouraged to experience serving other people with a variety of options. Radiate leadership intentionally moves to be on mission by making announcements, giving out flyers, and making posts on Facebook. When a student expresses an interest in serving, he or she is connected with the leader of that ministry.

Go

Radiate students get many opportunities to serve in the church and in the community. Teenagers actively serve in Radiate and many other areas, including the media department, landscaping team, the orchestra, and the children's department to keep children safe and dry.

Serving others is important, but reaching out to the community is a great responsibility and opportunity. According to Youth Pastor Brian Hanson, "There is nothing that energizes a group like wringing out the sponge of what they have learned."

Students capitalize on the opportunity to serve the community. One group of students loaded themselves with rakes, trash bags, and other tools to minister to people in need of yard work. As they walked door to door, they offered to do whatever was needed at the homes. When the work was finished, the team prayed with the homeowners and thanked them for the opportunity to serve.

Another team went on a battery outreach. Batteries were put in plastic bags with information about the church and distributed door to door. The team shared with those who came to the door that the batteries were for the smoke alarms in the house. The team met a need most people do not consider. The thoughtfulness proved to be well received.

Mission opportunities outside of the community are also available for students.

"Seekers" is an opportunity for high school students to serve at a summer camp for elementary children and do the ministry for a week. Students lead the chapel services, do maintenance and upkeep at the camp, and when possible, build relationships with the campers through activities.

Radiate also travels to Vancouver, British Columbia, to do missions with the Campbell River Tribe. The team builds relationships with the Indians and provides vacation Bible school and a basketball camp. Most of the tribe have never heard of Jesus, so the trip is of great importance. Sharing Jesus where His name isn't spoken is a powerful opportunity to let students experience the power of the gospel firsthand.

Foremost, students are continually reminded to do missions in their own lives. By living a godly life and inviting their friends to come to Radiate, the encouragement to be mission minded is lived out.

When students move through the process of Gospel, Grow, and Go, they are in the right place to be transformed. The programs never transform anyone, but they do create an environment for change to happen.

First Baptist Church, Oviedo, Florida

Emerge middle school ministry ministers to sixth-through eighth-grade students at First Baptist Church in Oviedo, Florida. The church averages twenty-six hundred people each weekend, including two hundred thirty middle school students.

Nathan Wilder, student pastor, was the catalyst for developing a discipleship process when he came to FBC Oviedo. After gaining approval from the executive staff, Nathan slowly began to implement the simple process in the middle school ministry. The senior pastor is now leading the church as a whole in implementing a strategic process, but the transition started in student ministry years before.

The vision of Emerge is to disciple teenagers to grow in a relationship with Jesus. Emerge's simple process displays its vision to produce maturing Christians: Middle School students will emerge into culture changers by being exposed to Jesus, being equipped to follow Jesus, and experiencing life serving Jesus.

When students attend a worship service, they are exposed to Jesus; when attending a small group, they are equipped to follow Him; and when serving others, they experience a life of serving Jesus.

Exposed to Jesus

Middle school students start showing up on Wednesdays about 5:30 p.m. in a shopping center near the church. They make their way inside to see which friends have already arrived and hang out until the service starts.

Just before 6 p.m., the students begin moving close to the stage where the band will be leading worship. The worship service is always energetic, resembling the adrenaline-filled teenagers who come to enjoy it. The games and skits bring a relational element to the service while the worship points students to God. After the band has finished, Pastor Nathan shares a talk from the Bible that includes a clear gospel presentation and gives the opportunity to respond.

After being dismissed from the worship service, students can go to a different area of the shopping center and enjoy the skate park, snack bar, and games. When it's time to leave at 8:30 p.m., students are still wanting more.

Emerge leadership is serious about discipling teenagers who will impact their world for Christ. However, spiritual growth will not continue by only attending Emerge; movement through the process must continue. Here are a few ways that Emerge is creating movement from the worship service to Bible Fellowship groups:

- Leaders of Bible Fellowship groups are asked to be present on Wednesday night to execute the "3 Cs" of Emerge: connecting with students, counseling the students, and performing crowd control. While at the Emerge service, the leaders are able to invite students to be part of the group they lead on Sunday morning.

- Announcements from the stage give clear direction how anyone can easily join a Bible Fellowship group.

- Students at Emerge can also check out "Ettachment" groups. These groups are held periodically on Wednesday nights to help a student experience what a small group looks and feels like before committing to go. After a teenager attends this group, a clear next step is provided for joining a Bible Fellowship group.

Equipped to Follow Jesus

Bible Fellowship groups are the second phase of the process and are offered three different times on Sunday morning. These groups are designed for students to be challenged to grow in their faith and build healthy friendships at the same time. Two or more friendly adults who love God lead each of these groups.

Teenagers come on Sunday morning to learn more about God's plan for their lives and the importance of spiritual disciplines. Students are challenged to have personal Bible study, pray daily, have accountability with a friend, and memorize Scripture.

Because Bible Fellowship groups stress relationships, groups are encouraged to spend time together outside of the regularly scheduled meeting time. Meaningful friendships can be developed when spending time together away from the church campus. Groups who are growing together are easy to spot; they have enjoyed some great experiences and have stories to prove it.

Bible Fellowship groups fulfill the *equipped* phase of the process. For continued movement to occur, Emerge uses creative steps to bridge students to the *experience* phase.

Bible Fellowship group leaders share the importance of putting faith to action and serving somewhere in the church. Occasionally Emerge places special emphasis on E-Teams (ministry teams) and gives options to serve. A teenager can join a ministry team at that time, reducing the number of steps to get involved in a ministry. Each of these actions, coupled with announcements from the stage and creative video reminders, make transitioning to serve easier.

The last phase of the process requires the most commitment: experiencing life serving Jesus.

Experience

"E-Teams" (ministry teams) provide opportunities for students to use their spiritual gifts, talents, and service to experience serving Jesus. For two hours on Sunday afternoons, the ministry teams meet at the church. The first thirty minutes of ministry team training is a challenge from the Bible. The students are then divided into three areas: creative arts, band, and outreach.

The creative arts team allows teenagers to serve by presenting media in Emerge, being part of the drama team, performing musically, or creating art for ministry use. The band gives opportunities for a teenager's musical talent to be used for God's glory.

Serving inside the church is important, but experiencing Jesus means serving outside of the church also. Outreach puts students on mission by making home visits, doing prayer walks, and practicing servant evangelism.

Mission trips are also offered as part of the *experience* phase of the process. Students who are involved are encouraged to attend Mission Camp.

Ministry wasn't always clearly defined at Emerge. Learning to say no to programs that don't fit its process led to the removing of two unnecessary programs: recreation night and a summer camp.

Recreation night was exactly as it sounds—a separate night of the week for hanging out at the church and playing sports. Recreation night was not attached to any other program in the process and did not encourage movement. In fact, the activity competed with the process as a priority, so the night of glorified babysitting was removed from the calendar.

Summer camp did not fit into the process either. Much time and money invested in a weeklong adventure that didn't encourage movement through the process proved wasteful. After much prayer and discussion, summer camp was also removed from the calendar.

Focus is important, but movement through the process is crucial for continued growth. Nathan Wilder explains why movement is critical:

> A student who only comes to Emerge will remain a baby Christian. A student who only comes to Bible Fellowship groups will never apply the truths he or she is learning. A student who only comes to E-Teams will not be serving with the love and power of Jesus.

Each program builds on the other, and together the process places a student on the path of discipleship. Because of such an experience-tested discipleship approach, Emerge Middle School ministry is seeing the fruit of their vision. Students are inviting Jesus into their lives and being transformed and impacting others!

Large-Church Research Thoughts

The student ministries that participated in the large-church case studies will be the first to tell you that their ministries aren't perfect. Each ministry is continually seeking new ways to execute better, communicate more clearly, and remove clutter that hinders movement.

However, these student ministries are using a discipleship process to lead students toward greater spiritual maturity. Although some of these ministries still have events, the ministries are not program driven, and the event is tied back into the process.

Our research also found the leaders of these ministries to be humble and genuinely passionate about students reaching their greatest potential in Christ. Although these men are leading large ministries, they are approachable and genuine.

We have learned lessons from these guys; they encouraged our student ministry to have honest discussion. Thank you, Dustin, Shawn, John, Bryan, and Nathan for your honesty and input in this project.

DISCUSSION QUESTIONS

1. What are two examples of movement in these studies? How is movement accomplished?
2. What are two examples of focus?
3. How does the programming focus in these ministries differ from our ministry?
4. What do we see as absent from the programming in these ministries?
5. What do these ministries have in common, if anything?

CHAPTER EIGHT

Parachurch Case Studies

"Go into all the world and preach
the gospel to the whole creation."

—Mark 16:15

T he Great Commission is simple: Go and make disciples.

Somewhere between Jesus' instruction on the mountain and our present culture, the church deviated from the mission to make disciples and became inward focused. Some churches found comfort in focusing on themselves. Other churches felt it was important to do what other churches were doing, and some churches focused on doing many good things, but advancing the gospel wasn't one of them.

Thus, the advent of the parachurch organization. When the local church shirked its responsibilities to effectively disciple teenagers, God raised up parachurch organizations.

The following two organizations are relentlessly sharing the gospel of Jesus and utilizing a process that moves teenagers deeper in spiritual maturity. Praise God for organizations that reach school campuses for the glory of God!

First Priority of South Florida

First Priority is a "Great Commission" organization that partners with local churches to reach middle school and high school campuses for Christ. The Equal Access Act passed by Ronald Reagan in 1984 gives Christian clubs the opportunity to meet on any public school campus in the United States.

First Priority is in many areas of the United States. The South Florida chapter has been uniting public school campuses with the church for the last eleven years. First Priority of South Florida has clubs on more than one hundred middle school and high school campuses across four counties in south Florida.

First Priority partners with local churches to identify key student leaders who have a burden to share Jesus at their school to start these clubs. Burdened to reach their friends for Christ, these teenagers are trained and developed as leaders of the club and make up the core launch team. In partnership with the local church, a Great Commission club is born.

First Priority clubs are student led with a campus coach (adult contributor) present. The campus coach is usually a youth pastor, ministry leader, or godly volunteer who is plugged into a local church. First Priority clubs meet either before school, during lunch periods, or after the school day is over. There are no meetings in the evenings or on weekends; only during or attached to the school day.

First Priority of South Florida's focus is to win teenagers to Christ on school campuses and place them into a local ministry for further discipleship. This vision is accomplished by using a four-step process. Each step represents one week and the entire process is repeated multiple times throughout the school year.

First Priority lives by these words: First Priority is committed to bridging the gap between young people and Jesus Christ by uniting the church to reach the campus!

First Priority uses the acronym T.E.A.M. to illustrate the process for reaching the school campuses.

Used by permission.

Fred Revell, campus ministry director for First Priority of South Florida, had this to say about the strategy:

> The vision of reaching students for Christ in multiple types of schools demands that the process be easily reproducible. The process is simple, but it is not

restrictive. The T.E.A.M. strategy can be used in both high schools and middle schools in any part of the country. While the club at every school will look different, the vision and the values remain the same.

Typically, this is where other Bible clubs miss the point. Many well-intentioned, God-loving teenagers meet faithfully every week but often are without direction. The Bible club functions like a smaller version of a church that is cluttered and unsure of how it will reach students for Christ.

The T.E.A.M. strategy is a platform to fulfill the vision God has given teenagers to reach their school for Christ. The process reduces the distractions. First Priority clubs say no to fund-raisers, T-shirt days, and mission trips. There are no meetings apart from school times and locations other than the school campus. All energy and focus are placed on school campuses, where students can be reached for Christ.

By utilizing the T.E.A.M. process, students are trained, encouraged, held accountable, and go on mission.

Training Week

The bell rings for lunch, and students begin making their way to the locker room across the campus. They aren't going for Phys. Ed., they are going to First Priority and since the football coach is the sponsor, they meet in his locker room. Other than the smell of feet and Axe body spray, the location is excellent.

The room is filled with excitement. "God did some amazing things in here last week," says Deanna, referring to three students who made decisions for Christ. The club will celebrate together and encourage the new believers, then prepare to do it all over again.

After a sophomore prays for the meeting time, Alex stands and nervously walks to the front of the room. This is only his second time speaking in the club, but he knows God wants him to share. He reads a few Scriptures and refers to the First Priority training guide for the month and shares how important it is to be a Christian both at church and at school.

After Alex finishes talking, the questions listed in the training guide are discussed. The discussion is good; students are being real about their struggles.

Training Week is used to teach the basics of the Christian faith. It's the perfect week for new believers; they learn more about their decision to follow Jesus and meet others who are growing in their faith.

Students who attend training week learn how to practically live out their faith. Encouragement Week is the next important step in clarifying the vision of the Great Commission club.

Encouragement Week

Students get spiritually pumped up at Encouragement Week. A guest speaker shares a short message from the

Bible that relates to staying focused on the mission of being a Great Commission club.

This week the guest speaker is a former weight lifter and football player; his body mass alone is reason to stop and stare. The speaker shares passionately with the club about keeping focused on the goal of winning friends to Christ. He draws a few analogies from his college football days to make the point. The talk is inspiring and effective; students are ready to charge hell with a squirt gun.

Sometimes, instead of a guest speaker, a teenager will share testimony of how he came to Christ. The weeks when someone who became a Christian in the First Priority club shares his testimony are especially encouraging.

Encouragement week finishes with students praying for each other and plans to meet for Accountability Week.

Accountability Week

The three main focuses of Accountability Week are: pray, plan, and perform.

The *prayer* phase of accountability week is a designated time of prayer for unsaved friends. Each student receives a business-size First Priority prayer card with spaces for five names. The purpose is to write down the name of five friends who need a relationship with Jesus and pray that week for their salvation. The club also prays for the courage and the opportunity to invite friends to next week's meeting when the gospel will be clearly presented.

The reverse side of the prayer card serves as a form of accountability for spiritual health. As Christians, students know they are accountable for their walk with God. As part of a Great Commission club committed to winning their school for Christ, members are also accountable to each other.

Here are the questions for spiritual inventory:

1. How is your communication with God?
2. Are you reading your Bible?
3. Are you having your quiet time?
4. Is your conduct reflective of your walk with God?
5. Have you invited the five people you listed on this card?

These questions are fundamental for accountability and verify that spiritual disciplines are being practiced.

The *plan* phase is the preparation for Mission Week. Students volunteer for leadership roles that include being the emcee, leading in prayer, being a greeter, or handing out pizza.

The *perform* phase holds students accountable to serve their school. After checking with school administration to be sure their plans are approved, the love of Jesus is shared with no strings attached.

One club came up with the idea of passing out Krispy Kreme doughnuts at their school's main entrance as students arrived for the day. Half-awake teenagers were surprised and thankful for the heavy dose of sugar for first period. As the doughnuts were passed out, the First Priority invite cards with club time and location were given also. As a result of the doughnuts specifically, a junior came to Mission Week and gave his heart to Jesus.

Other clubs have handed out cold water with First Priority club information on each bottle. After a long day of classes, the free gift is readily accepted. The random act of kindness motivates even the shyest freshman to ask, "Why are you doing this?"

First Priority clubs are convinced they can show the love of Jesus in these simple ways. Training Week, Encouragement Week, and Accountability Week lead up to the final club meeting in the process: Mission Week.

Mission Week

Dave's walk to the locker room takes a few moments longer than usual this week. He keeps stopping to invite the friends he sees on his way to Mission Week for free pizza and soda. When asked, "What's it for?" he answers honestly and assures them they will have a good time. By the time Dave gets to the locker room, three of his friends are with him. After being greeted at the door, they arrive in the room shortly before the meeting starts.

Tommy, a sophomore from Dave's church, volunteered to be the emcee for the day. He leads the group through an icebreaker that gets everyone laughing and wondering how Sprite and bananas could make such a mess. When the laughter settles down, Tommy takes time to introduce the guest speaker.

The guest speaker is the youth pastor of one of the guys in the First Priority Club. The next few moments is what all of the planning, praying, and inviting have been for: the opportunity for a friend to hear the gospel clearly.

The speaker passionately and clearly shares a story from the book of Mark about how a man's life was changed after meeting Jesus. Students are moved after hearing that there is a God who loves them and wants to know them. After explaining what it means to have a relationship with Jesus, the speaker allows for a time of response. "If you would like to talk to someone about how to have a relationship with God, raise your hand. We'll talk after we pray."

A friend of Dave's raises his hand. *Wow. It's really happening*, Dave thinks to himself.

During a time of commitment, the speaker explains to Dave's friend how to have a relationship with Jesus. In the next few moments, a life is changed for eternity. Before heading back to class, the friend fills out a spiritual birth certificate and is given his first Bible.

Dave will follow up and invite his friend to church to get him in a place where he can begin to grow. Dave also invites his friend back to First Priority for next week, Training Week, to get to know more people and begin learning more of God's Word.

This four-week process is repeated multiple times throughout the year. Although Mission Week is named at the end of the process, it also serves as the entry point because the process is continuous.

First Priority uses a discipleship process to reach students on public school campuses for Christ by utilizing the T.E.A.M. strategy.

> Coming into high school, I got involved in a homosexual relationship. Deep in my heart I knew I didn't want to live in that lifestyle. I broke off the relationship and was trying to overcome something I couldn't overcome on my own.

> At the end of my sophomore year, I attended First Priority. The speaker gave the gospel and gave us an opportunity to respond. I got up out of my seat and gave my heart to the Lord. Now, as a college student, God is giving me the opportunity to share my testimony in other high schools. —Ronel

Young Life, Naperville, Illinois

Young Life began with a desire to reach local teenagers for Christ in a 1940s small Texas town. Today Young Life estimates it will impact more than six hundred sixty thousand students around the world this year.

Young Life currently has a presence in all fifty states and in fifty-three other countries. For this case study, we will focus on the Young Life in Naperville, Illinois.

Rob Hankins, area director for Young Life, Naperville, fully believes that relationships are the key to reaching students. Everything at Young Life is done in the context of relationships. The programs that Young Life use are simply a means to build relationships that will display God's love.

Young Life's mission is introducing adolescents to Jesus Christ and helping them grow in their faith. In order to build spiritually into the lives of teenagers, Young Life uses a process that consists of three programs: Club, Campaigner, and Work Crew.

Club

Football practice just finished, and it's 7:30 p.m. Todd quickly runs to the locker room to clean up and realizes he has about thirty minutes to shower, pick up his two buddies, and get to Club on time. No sweat.

As Todd climbs into the 1984 Plymouth his dad gave him, he prays for a moment for what could happen tonight. He's invited his friends to Club a few times before and this week they've finally agreed to come.

The guys arrive at the house where Club is held a few minutes early and make their way to the basement where everyone is hanging out. As he watches his friends take in what's happening, Todd pauses for a moment to pray again. *God, would You touch their hearts tonight? Please . . .*

A guy with a guitar leads everyone in a couple of songs that are familiar and easy to sing. After the music, a girl Todd met two weeks ago leads a game that involves four people, a whoopee cushion, and a bag of French fries. The guys nearly fall off their chairs from laughing so hard. They never saw *that* coming.

Without an introduction, the Young Life leader walks to the front of the room and begins to share a story from his high school days. The speaker told of his football career and the scholarships that were available. Unfortunately a knee surgery left him flat on his back and without hope for an education.

Despite the disappointment, the speaker shared how he found hope again in a relationship with Christ. Although his athletic career was over, his life had just begun. The talk ends with the speaker sharing how everyone can start a new life in Christ.

On the drive home, Todd's friend begins to ask a few questions. He liked what he heard and wants to know more about having a relationship with Christ.

Club is an exciting outreach program where students are encouraged to come and bring their non-Christian friends. The Club program consists of three basic elements that engage students to be open to the gospel: music, humor, and a message.

Live, upbeat singing is part of the Club experience. Secular music might be played, but the songs are meaningful and will echo with what is happening in the life of a teenager. There are also games and skits to encourage laughter at situations, but not at other people.

Club facilitates relationship building, and most importantly, is a place where students hear how to have a relationship with Jesus. Students who make a decision for Christ at Club are encouraged to keep attending and to grow in their faith. Ideally, a friend will invite the new Christian to go to church.

Students who attend Club are also encouraged to move to the Bible study phase of the process, Campaigners.

Campaigners

Nine high school students sit in a circle on the floor and listen to their Young Life leader explain the Scripture that was read in Romans 12. Before tonight, most of them were unsure about what it means to be a "living sacrifice." After a few questions and some great answers, heads start to nod along in agreement. A lightbulb is going off. They are beginning to understand.

This is Campaigners, the sequential next step for discipleship at Young Life.

Bible study and leadership development are the key areas in this program. Campaigners is not like the Club program; the primary focus is to study God's Word and apply the truths to everyday life.

Young Life, Naperville also develops potential leaders at the Campaigner level. These young leaders are held personally accountable for the spiritual direction of their lives. These leaders are encouraged to have an accountability partner and continue growing in their relationship with God on their own.

Teenagers who are Christians and have been involved with Campaigners are challenged to move to the next phase of discipleship, the Work Crew.

Work Crew

Cleaning up after other people is no fun. Scrubbing dirty toilets at a summer camp isn't glorious at all. For one month, a student will leave home to serve others who are enjoying a week of fun and sunshine. Believe it or not, this is the next level of discipleship, the Work Crew.

Work Crew is a great opportunity to experience what it means to serve. For many teenagers, Work Crew is their first opportunity to serve Christ by serving other people. The month of sweat isn't only about learning humility; the time away from home is very formational in their walk with God.

Each student is assigned to work under a Work Crew boss. Don't picture an older, gruff-looking man with a cigar who yells all the time, but rather a loving Young Life leader who will pour personally into each worker. Personal, intentional discipleship takes place at Work Camp, coupled with the opportunity to learn real servanthood.

Work Crew is an essential part of discipleship for Young Life, Naperville. Those who are growing in their faith must be given opportunities to live out what they have learned. Working at a camp in the summer and building into the lives of others are an effective means of discipleship.

When students who are seniors return from Work Crew, they are considered leaders at the Club and Campaigners level. Their new responsibility is to invest in other students.

Young Life, Naperville understands the importance of moving teenagers forward in their relationship with God. Club is a great place to build relationships and hear the truth about Jesus. Campaigners continues to put students in the path of spiritual growth by consistent, meaningful Bible study, and Work Crew gives the opportunity to live out their faith and experience the life Jesus intended.

Rob Hankins isn't merely the area director for Young Life, Naperville; he's also a product of Young Life. Rob gave his heart to Jesus while being involved with Young Life as a teenager.

Rob loves working for Young Life because he sees the process at work and making a difference in the lives of teenagers. There is no pressure to keep people happy, only a constant pursuit of seeing students won to Jesus. When asked why Rob appreciated how Young Life disciples students, he responded,

> Young Life's methods of meeting students where they are is consistent with how Jesus did ministry. Jesus didn't stay in one place and tell the people to come to Him; He went to where they were.

Here are a few short testimonies from students across the United States about Young Life.

> When I was in high school, I can remember Young Life being a safe place to go whenever I needed to get away from the pressures of being a teenager. What

meant the most, though, was that the leaders were always interested in me, and it really made me feel like someone cared. That's what Young Life is all about. —Shannon

After meeting my local area director, it was one of the first times I witnessed an unconditional love in human form. —Casey

Young Life let me associate Jesus with friends and fun. —Michael

Praise God for ministries that will go where the students are and win them to Christ! First Priority and Young Life are designed around a simple process. Local churches can learn a lot from the strategic focus of these parachurch organizations.

DISCUSSION QUESTIONS

1. What instances of clarity, movement, alignment, and focus do you see in these two organizations?
2. Why would having a clearly defined process be instrumental when reaching school campuses?
3. If parachurch organizations are supported by donations, how would a clear discipleship process be useful?
4. What lessons can the local church student ministries learn from parachurch organizations?

CHAPTER NINE

Small and Midsize Church Case Studies

There are no small churches,
just small people.

—Edwin Louis Cole

M oses stood in front of the burning bush and fumbled with his words. His curiosity led him to look at the bush that wasn't being consumed and soon he was engaged in face-to-face conversation with the Almighty (see Exod. 3).

God shared with Moses His desire to see His people freed from the hand of the Egyptians. Shortly after that, God told Moses that he would be an integral part of that process. The shoeless Moses was insecure and couldn't envision being the leader of God's people.

But I AM a nobody. Who would listen to me?

I will be with you.

But what if they ask who sent me?

Tell them I AM has sent me to you. (author paraphrase)

Moses had some great excuses, but God lovingly assured Moses that he would lead the children of Israel. I AM was going to enable and empower Moses to complete the task.

Moses trusted I AM, and a life of serving God was born.

Over his lifetime, God used Moses to do amazing things and continually affirmed to Moses that His words were true.

Student ministries can be guilty of having a Moses mind-set.

Regardless of how many kids show up at your services, the number of volunteers you have or the size of your budget, God wants to use you to do amazing things in the lives of students. Like Moses, we sometimes give God reasons why we can't disciple students the way we think discipleship should be done. *We don't have the people or the resources. We aren't that creative. Who will help me?*

Fortunately the vision God gave you to disciple students is not limited to the size of your student ministry. Fulfilling God's plan for your ministry is difficult if you compare your ministry to another ministry. Comparison is never fair. Or healthy.

Regardless of the size, many student ministries have implemented a simple process and are pursuing the vision God has given them to disciple teenagers. Because simple student ministry is not a model, a discipleship process can be developed for any ministry regardless of location, resources, worship preference, or size.

Discipleship occurs when leaders are intentional about seeing student's lives transformed and have implemented a plan to disciple.

Life Journey Christian Church, Bakersfield, California

The Peak is the ministry to teenagers of Life Journey Church. Approximately eighty people attend the weekend service of Life Journey Church and twenty-five students attend the midweek service. Life Journey Christian Church meets in a rented, light-industrial space. On Sunday the entire church meets in the space, but on Wednesday night it becomes The Peak.

Volunteers have always led The Peak. These faithful adults oversee the ministry including the worship service, small groups, and service opportunities. The pastor of Life Journey Christian Church, David Limiero, holds the volunteers accountable.

The Peak believes students have the best opportunity to grow spiritually by moving through its discipleship process: *Celebrate, Connect, and Contribute.*

Simple Student Ministry

Students celebrate by attending a worship service, connect by joining a small group, and contribute by giving of themselves to minister to others.

Celebrate

Michael's stomach won't quit rumbling. It's time to eat.

This is the first Wednesday of the month, which means there is free food. After a couple of quick shots on the basketball court, Michael makes his way into the building to see what's happening.

To his delight, volunteers have a huge pile of tacos and a dozen two-liter bottles of caffeinated beverage on the table. A moment later, a leader prays for the food and Michael heads outside with a plate of tacos to eat with a couple of friends.

The guys manage to finish the tacos in record time and shoot a few more balls before being told the celebration service is about to begin. The guys make their way inside, only slightly sweaty from the quick game of shootout.

After calling everyone to come closer to the stage, the worship leader begins to pray that God will do some amazing things in the service. With that, a guitar begins to play and soon, students are worshipping God.

As the band plays, many of the students are enjoying time in God's presence. Michael looks around the room and thinks to himself, *It is obvious students came to celebrate.* Even though the worship set lasted longer than usual, the

■ 184 ■

students are ready for more. However, the worship leader prays one more time, then asks students to take a seat.

The volunteer with tonight's message walks to the front and shares a powerful message from 1 Timothy. He challenges the students to run from the traps of the world and to keep fighting the good fight. "I needed to hear that," Michael confesses to a friend. "My life has been messed up lately."

The celebration service comes to a close after another song and sharing Communion. As Michael leaves the service, he sighs because he has some thinking to do. He is encouraged, however, that God is shaping him into His image.

The first Wednesday night of the month consists of food, worship, and teaching. The other three weeks of the month no food is served and the first thirty minutes of the service is devoted to celebration and worship. Students spend the remaining two hours connecting in small groups.

Connect

Small groups at The Peak are arranged by gender, but are open to both middle school and high school students. Because they immediately follow the celebration service, small groups are almost always 100 percent of the worship service attendance.

The purpose of a small group is for students to grow in their relationship with God and with other Christians.

Each week small groups cover one chapter of the curriculum they are studying. The leader facilitates questions and makes personal application toward the students' lives; these times of discussion are so much more productive than just sitting face forward in a chair.

Occasionally, a small group will hold students accountable through the use of RPMS. These are bold questions about how each person is doing relationally, physically, mentally, and spiritually. Although difficult to answer sometimes, the questions remind the group that spiritual growth is important for each and they are accountable.

Small groups also allow students time to pray for their lost friends. Each person in the group is encouraged to name someone who needs Christ and together the group prays for the people mentioned. Michael, a student at The Peak, calls it "evangelistic praying."

At the conclusion of the small group, the students return to the worship area to share Communion and sing a couple more songs.

After being involved with worship and small groups, students are encouraged by leaders to put their faith into action by serving others.

Contribute

Students serve in various capacities in the church. Because of the size of Life Journey, students and adults often serve together. Students participate in the worship band, both in the student service and the adult service. Occasionally a band consisting of only teenagers will lead the adult worship service. Students perform setup and teardown, clean up, and serve in the preschool ministry so parents can enjoy the service.

Students also participate in missions. Life Journey Christian Church focuses many efforts on a low-income housing neighborhood in a nearby community. Teenagers get to show the love of Jesus a couple of times per year by being involved with events at the housing community.

On a "Gone for Good" Sunday, students and adults join forces to serve somewhere in the community. The regularly scheduled worship service becomes an opportunity to serve others outside the church. Those who attend Gone for Good enjoy worship and a short Bible study before leaving on mission. After going into the community to show the love of Jesus, the group enjoys lunch to celebrate what they have experienced.

Students live out the process when they attend a celebration service, go to a small group, and reach out to others. In spite of the fact that fewer than one hundred people attend Life Journey every week, the student ministry pursues intentional discipleship by utilizing a simple process.

And we applaud the relentless focus of the volunteers who are effectively ministering to teenagers.

When asked how having a discipleship process has influenced the student ministry, Pastor David Limiero responded by saying, "Clarity is the big thing. It is so easy to overcomplicate discipleship. It's hard to make discipleship simple. A process makes that possible."

Shively Baptist Church, Louisville, Kentucky

Encounter 463 is the student ministry of Shively Baptist Church. The church averages five hundred seventy-five people in attendance for its weekend service, including seventy teenagers each week.

Phil Rice, student pastor, developed and implemented a discipleship process in early 2007. While the entire church is moving toward a simple process, the student ministry leads the way in reducing complexity.

Leadership at Encounter understands the busy life of a teenager. Encounter has no extra programs or events. Although many creative ideas for activities are brought to leadership each year, anything that does not fit in the process is never allowed to start. The time saved from a busy calendar is spent developing excellence in areas of essential ministry.

The process for Encounter was birthed out of the vision God gave the leadership to disciple students. Special emphasis is placed on relationship building, evangelism, Bible study, leadership development, and leadership reproduction.

Leadership took these five core values and synthesized them into the *Connect, Grow, Go* process. Students move through the process by attending a worship service, going to small group, and serving others inside and outside the church.

Connect

Jodi and her friends arrive at Encounter 463. After a long day of school, the girls are looking forward to hanging out together tonight and hearing more of the "Grace" series they've been studying. Because the middle school service meets at this time, the three friends make their way to the Family Life Center until their worship service begins at 7 p.m.

Jodi gets a drink from the snack bar as a group of guys start playing basketball on the court. After getting comfortable, the girls begin talking about a science test and somehow end up discussing how long a pair of socks should really last.

They've talked almost the entire hour, and though the conversation wasn't that serious, the friends have enjoyed spending time together. Realizing how long they've been talking, they move quickly from the Family Life Center to the youth area. The service always starts at 7 p.m., and missing the worship band is never cool.

Jodi pauses for a moment during the first song to soak in the words. More than ever, she realizes how God has transformed her this past year. She's been given some great experiences to grow and trust God.

After the worship set is finished, one of the leaders walks on stage to share a few announcements. Among those is an opportunity to be part of a mission trip; she went last year and loved it. There was also a challenge to show up on Sunday for small groups. *Oh yeah,* Jodi thinks, *I should invite these girls to small groups with me.*

The series on "Grace" has been great and tonight is no different. After looking around, most of the students seemed to be very engaged with the content of the message.

As the worship service comes to a close, Jodi begins to reflect on the evening. It's been a good night. The service was great and Jodi learned a few things. As she walks out the doors, she thinks to herself, *I love this place.*

This is a typical Wednesday night at the Encounter worship service. The names may be different, but the scenario plays out often. Middle school and high school meet at the same time in different areas, then switch locations for worship and hang-out time.

Students who attend the Encounter worship service enjoy meeting new friends and learning more about God. Students are encouraged both in person and by announcements to move to the next phase of discipleship, small groups.

Grow

Jodi remembered on Saturday night to invite two of her friends to D Groups on Sunday morning. Only one of the girls could come, and this will give them a chance to talk while driving to D Groups.

Jodi likes going to D Groups, but she will be the first to say that teenagers are tough to motivate if they wake up too early. Her D Group leader makes it easier to get out of bed.

Her D Group leader has been a big part of Jodi's life for the last two years. In difficult times, she has helped her to understand some of the issues in her life. The Bible study is pretty good too. The girls in the group enjoy the conversation; having a small-group leader who can lead discussion really makes a big difference.

Small groups are called "D Groups" or "Discipleship Groups" and match the *grow* phase of the process. D Groups are offered two different times on Sunday.

The first opportunity to attend D Groups is on Sunday morning. Since the adult ministries still use the Sunday school format, many teenagers are on the church campus and can attend D Groups.

The second opportunity to attend D Groups is on Sunday night. These groups are offered after other programming but provide an option for those who can't make it earlier.

D Group leaders are encouraged to build lasting relationships with students. When a group spends time together outside of D Groups, their friendship grows. Groups who are growing spiritually and in friendship provide a powerful influence in the life of a student. Once students are attending the worship service and in a small group, they are encouraged to serve others.

Go

Serving others includes weekly and yearly opportunities for students to experience what they've been hearing in all of the teaching.

Students serve others in the church by being on a ministry team. These students serve as greeters, play in the band, take attendance at Encounter, or serve in other areas around the campus. However, ministry team members don't just serve; they are trained to be leaders.

On Sunday nights team members receive specific training. Greeters are taught why it's important to make guests feel welcome. The worship band is not only taught how to be better musicians but how to lead worship with integrity. Occasionally a student is taught to communicate effectively and share a message from the Bible at the Encounter service.

Ministry teams help to develop a serving mind-set. However, Encounter 463 wants more for students than only ministering inside the church; students should also share their faith out in the community. Once a year Encounter 463 challenges students to pick up a hammer and hopefully, change a life through their involvement in missions.

When students attend the Encounter service, go to a D Group, and serve others, Encounter 463 believes they are in the best possible environments to mature in their relationship with Christ.

DISCUSSION QUESTIONS

1. What are some advantages of discipling students in a small church? What are some disadvantages?
2. What lessons can we learn from these churches?
3. How does being simple help reduce the amount of resources a student ministry usually needs?
4. What are the similarities between the large-church, small-church, and parachurch studies?
5. Did any of the case studies stand out for a particular reason? If so, why?

CHAPTER TEN

The Transition to Simple

Change is hard because people overestimate the value of
what they have—and underestimate the value of what they
may gain by giving that up.

—James Belasco and Ralph Strayer

T he religious people were upset. Levi, a former tax
collector and new disciple of Jesus, was throwing a
huge dinner party at his house in celebration of his
new faith. Levi invited his tax collector friends to come and
spend time with Jesus.

While Jesus and the guys were eating, a few Pharisees
began to complain to Jesus' disciples about the fact He was
eating and spending time with sinners. Overhearing the
conversation, Jesus quickly clarified His purpose for not
only eating with the tax collectors but for His presence on
earth altogether: "The healthy don't need a doctor, but the

sick do. I have not come to call the righteous, but sinners to repentance" (Luke 5:31–32).

Problem solved, so it would seem. However, the legalists persisted. "How is it that we fast, but your disciples do not fast?" (Luke 5:33, author's paraphrase).

The Pharisees were perfectionists in keeping the Law and watched Jesus carefully for any opportunity to discredit Him. These men had been dedicated to fasting twice a week (see Luke 18:12) and wondered why Jesus and His disciples didn't practice the same spiritual disciplines.

Jesus knew that fasting wasn't the real issue as the questions were only symptoms of a deeper spiritual problem. As He had done many times before, Jesus answered the questions in the form of a parable.

> "And no one puts new wine into old wineskins. Otherwise, the new wine will burst the skins, it will spill, and the skins will be ruined. But new wine should be put into fresh wineskins. And no one, after drinking old wine, wants new, because he says, 'The old is better.'" (Luke 5:37–39)

Wineskins were usually made from the skin of a goat. When wine was poured into these skins, the fermentation process would begin. After a few days, the skin that held the wine would begin to change as the gases and juices of fermentation weakened the bag of skin. An attempt to pour new wine into a bag of fermented wine would break the bag and ruin both sets of wine.

Jesus taught His interrogators an important lesson. Jesus did not come to be subject to religious preferences and His mission would not be hindered by man-made rules. He did not come to abolish the Law, but to fulfill the requirements of the Law in us through His righteousness. Christ's perfect sacrifice on the cross fulfilled the Law.

Student ministries are often guilty of attempting to put new wine into old wineskins. We want God to bring transformation in our students, but we refuse to change how we disciple students. Values such as students engaging in missions and nurturing relationships with godly adults do not fit into a complicated wineskin of student ministry. When our traditions or programming take priority over discipleship, we have said no to new wine.

If we attempt to cram a renewed heart for student discipleship into the old paradigm, we are adding new wine to old wineskins. The old ministry paradigm can't handle more.

A new wineskin is necessary.

The time has come to trade the wineskin of complicated programming for a discipleship process that's clear and easy to follow. Intentional discipleship must become the new wineskin. The overprogrammed calendar has to go. We must begin to remove the clutter so that clear and understandable discipleship can take place.

But a new wineskin will be a change, and change is difficult. Transition is never simple. Student ministries often set the pace for change in churches. Change is sometimes expected in student ministry. And with students constantly graduating and a new crop of students entering the student ministry, change in student ministry is often more easily executed than in the larger church body.

Perhaps you're a student ministry leader in a church that's extremely unfocused, and God will use the new wineskins in the student ministry to initiate change in the church as a whole. Pray that God will use your passion, vision, and creativity to begin to stir a desire for change in your entire church.

Every ministry is unique and faces different challenges. Issues such as the speed of change in your culture, the change receptivity of the church, your tenure as a leader, and the priority placed on student ministry all play into the difficult challenge of transitioning to a simple philosophy of student ministry.

The variety of factors impacting the ability to instigate change in a variety of contexts makes writing about change equally challenging. Leadership is often about change, and leadership is an art. Not a science. So while there are some overarching change principles, leading change is an art. However, we will wrap up *Simple Student Ministry* with some practical and overarching steps to transition to a simple and strategic process.

Evaluate

Leading significant change takes time. Don't rush into any changes immediately. As Nehemiah walked around his city evaluating the broken walls, observe the programs and events you currently offer and evaluate your ministry. Record where your time and your volunteers' time is spent. Don't assume you know everything about each program; assess and ask bold questions.

A humbling but practical way of evaluating is to speak to students who have graduated from your ministry. Ask them for an honest evaluation of their experience in your ministry. *What was missing? What could we have done better? Do you feel you were spiritually prepared to leave the student ministry?*

As you observe and evaluate, constantly remember the desire God has given you to see student's lives transformed. This is not a time to beat yourself up; instead, this is a time for change. Without the sense of frustration and holy dissatisfaction, change will not occur. If the observation leads you to your knees in prayer and weeping, good things are ahead.

Leading change will test your leadership abilities. You will be stretched. You will get tired. You will probably be emotionally, physically, and spiritually drained. A leader who recognizes God as his only source of strength will continue to lead courageously.

Pray Often

David, king of Israel and giant killer, made his share of mistakes. Most leaders in student ministry wouldn't want adultery and murder to cover up the adultery on their résumé. Those records would probably hinder landing a job in student ministry.

However, other characteristics about David stand out. David killed a lion and a bear with his hands. He slew a giant with a rock and a slingshot. When David could have seized an opportunity to extract revenge on Saul for trying to kill him, he submitted to God and allowed Saul to leave the cave unharmed. As a warrior and a king, David led armies to battle and won great victories in the name of the Lord. David was courageous, loyal to authority, and humble in the presence of God. Most importantly, David knew how to pray.

When David prayed, he prayed specifically for the situations that faced him. He prayed for wisdom. He begged God for mercy and forgiveness. He poured his heart out completely to God.

> I cry aloud to the LORD; I plead aloud to the LORD for mercy. I pour out my complaint before Him; I reveal my trouble to Him. Although my spirit is weak within me, You know my way. Along this path I travel they have hidden a trap for me. (Ps. 142:1–3)

If you are ready to lead change, you must seek God's face often. E. M. Bounds said, "We pray as we live; we live as we pray." Prayer has a profound effect on how we live our lives and how we lead others. Your time in your prayer closet will be reflected in how you lead change.[1]

Petition God specifically about issues you are facing. Pray for wisdom for the programs that best place students on the path to experience transformation. Pray for the leaders and students by name. Pray for the hearts of leadership to develop a greater hunger for students to be discipled. Pray that you will be faithful and courageous as a leader.

Be Humble

Jim Collins, author and teacher to senior executives at more than one hundred corporations, defines five levels of leadership from his extensive research of companies. Each level of leadership is significant to both the professional and personal characteristics of a great leader. While the levels of leadership vary, the level five leader is one who is humble yet utilizes professional will to get the job done.

Collins's research shows that, even in business, one characteristic of the most effective leaders is genuine humility. These leaders are not out to make a name for themselves, but instead are consumed with the success of their company.[2]

Humility is a characteristic of a great leader in business. More importantly, humility is a characteristic of a leader of God's people. Genuine humility reduces the confidence in ourselves and places our confidence where it belongs, in God. God values humility as demonstrated in these verses:

My hand made all these things, and so they all came into being. [This is] the LORD's declaration. I will look favorably on this kind of person: one who is humble, submissive in spirit, and who trembles at My word. (Isa. 66:2)

The fear of the LORD is wisdom's instruction, and humility comes before honor. (Prov. 15:33)

But He gives greater grace. Therefore He says: God resists the proud but gives grace to the humble. (James 4:6)

Moses, one of the greatest leaders in the Bible, possessed great humility. His great leadership was in direct proportion to his humility. "Moses was a very humble man, more so than any man on the face of the earth" (Num. 12:3).

Moses led over a million Israelites out of Egyptian captivity. Notice how the most humble man on the planet motivated God's people to trust God and cross the Red Sea.

But Moses said to the people, "Don't be afraid. Stand firm and see the LORD's salvation He will provide for you today; for the Egyptians you see today, you will never see again. The LORD will fight for you; you must be quiet." (Exod. 14:13–14)

Moses's humility in leadership allowed him to place his confidence in the power of God. The seeds of humility were planted in Moses way back at the burning bush when God assured Moses that I AM would handle business. Moses knew the tasks ahead were too big for him, yet he was willing to lead others because of who God was.

If you find the challenges you face difficult, you're in good company. The apostle Paul felt this way too. Comfort can be found in Paul's second letter to the Corinthians.

> But He said to me, "My grace is sufficient for you,
> for power is perfected in weakness." Therefore, I will
> most gladly boast all the more about my weaknesses,
> so that Christ's power may reside in me. (2 Cor. 12:9)

Humility is necessary during times of change in student ministry. Humility shows that your greatest desire is for God to be great in the lives of the students you lead. Humility reveals that your ultimate desire is not to be the most liked or the coolest student ministry leader, but your desire is the transformation of the students to whom God has entrusted you.

Be Patient with People

Patience may be a virtue, but patience can be lost quite easily in certain situations. In the grocery store, the cashier behind the counter who is on her cell phone instead of checking out the customers can anger the most patient. Sometimes your testimony may be the only thing that keeps you from getting upset when she gives you that look that you are "interrupting" her private time.

At Taco Bell, there is the guy who has been standing in line for ten minutes, and now that he's at the register, he finally decides to look at the menu. Tacos would be too easy; he is all about the chalupa, no guacamole with extra onion. *Yeah, whatever, Rachel Ray, just get out of the way.*

You will probably enjoy similar what-the-heck-is-happening-here situations when transitioning a ministry around a simple process. A deeper and more considerate patience will be required of you during times of change.

After you have finished explaining the process for the twenty-sixth time in nine days, a leader might say, "What do you mean we aren't going to keep having students to the church on Friday night for peanut brittle and Red Rover? Are you trying to get them to start using drugs?"

You must exercise great patience with people who are slow to change. Many people have never experienced significant change inside the church. Unfortunately you may hear the seven words of every dying ministry that refuses to change: *We've never done it that way before!*

Spend time lovingly sharing why the ministry philosophy must change for God's best to be realized. These conversations will require a patience that only God can provide. Patience is not only a godly character trait, but is also a very helpful relational tool.

> The end of a matter is better than its beginning;
> a patient spirit is better than a proud spirit.
> (Eccles. 7:8)

A hot-tempered man stirs up dissension, but a patient man calms a quarrel. (Prov. 15:18 NIV)

A patient person shows great understanding, but a quick-tempered one promotes foolishness. (Prov. 14:29)

When you are patient in times of heated debate or questioning, your patience will help calm the situation. Your patience will allow for honest discussion and dialogue to take place. And honest discussion will lead to greater ownership among the people involved in your ministry. Be patient with people, yet be urgent in communication.

Urgent in Communication

You must create a sense of urgency for change in your student ministry. The urgency isn't recklessness, but rather uneasiness about the way discipleship is designed and executed. Urgency gives the sense, *we can't continue ministry as usual. The clock is ticking and we must change the way we disciple students.*

Urgency drives people from their comfort zones and enables them to see the big picture. Without urgency, you will hear the phrase, *If it ain't broke, why fix it?* There will be no understanding of the necessity to change because the problem with current discipleship hasn't been established. The need for urgency can be established by answering a few questions honestly.

Are we effectively leading students to Christ? How are we doing at discipling those who make a decision for Christ? What kind of spiritually growing student are we producing? Can we even articulate clearly how we are designed to disciple students?

Pose these questions to godly leaders, and their evaluation will begin. As you evaluate in community, the holy dissatisfaction will create urgency. As a team, design the discipleship process for your student ministry. Let's summarize the four key elements of a simple process.

1. Design a Simple Process (Clarity)

Before a house is built, you must first design the blueprints. Blueprints are drawn on paper before a cinderblock is laid or a hammer is swung. As you discuss the blueprint for your student ministry, you are not yet making changes programmatically. You are simply determining the type of student that God has given you a vision to produce.

As you begin, mentally suspend reality. Lay the existing programming to the side. Forget the events, the yearly conferences, and cluttered calendar. Design with a blank sheet of paper.

Seek God's face as to *what* type of student disciple would honor Him. Investigate Scripture. Let God's Word weave a stronger view of who a disciple is and how true discipleship is fleshed out in everyday life.

Discuss *what* a student disciple in your ministry context looks like. Define the type of student you hope to produce. As a team, describe a student disciple in the context of your ministry in three to four phases.

Many characteristics of a disciple can be combined into one overarching thought. For example, the terms "growing spiritually, being holy, and loving Jesus more every day" could be summed up by the word *grow*. This is true for each aspect of the process. Remember, a short and succinct process statement is easier to remember.

After prayer and discussion, you should be able to fill in the following statement concerning what defines a disciple in the context of your student ministry.

Disciples in our student ministry: _____, _____, _____, and _____.

These blanks represent the type of spiritually maturing student your ministry desires to develop.

Next, you must discern *how* you are going to disciple these students. After reviewing the definitions of a disciple, place the phrases in sequential order. Place the definitions of discipleship in order from the least level of commitment to the greatest level of commitment.

Discern what aspect of discipleship usually occurs first. For instance, before a student grows in serving Christ, he must have a relationship with Him. Being sequential allows students to move forward in very clear steps.

Your purpose should be a process. The words and number of words used in the previous statement should be the same. You are simply crafting the order. Using the above words, fill in these blanks using process terms:

Students become mature disciples in our student ministry by

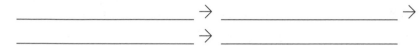

This is your process. This is *how* the team agrees that disciples are made in your student ministry. Everything done up to this point is the blueprint. No demolition of programs or events has taken place.

Discuss your process with others. As students and leaders begin to understand the importance of a discipleship process, the need for the right programs to move students through the process will become clearer.

2. Place Key Programs along the Process (Movement)

Choose one essential program for each phase in the process. Remember, these programs should be specifically designed to match that particular phase in the process. A current program may work after you have changed or tweaked the focus. Or you may need to create and implement an entirely new program.

As you consider which program to place along each stage of your process, ask your team which program is the best environment to place students for each phase of the process to occur. View programs as tools to move students through the process of discipleship.

This step will introduce change to people. With each following step, more change will be introduced. Your process has only been conceptual until now.

The first program should be the entry point in your process. This is the program when guests usually come and students invite their friends. This program should be the program requiring the lowest level of commitment.

Each additional program should match the increasing levels of commitment in your process. Movement best happens when programming is sequential and moves students spiritually deeper in their faith. After you have finished this step, you should be able to fill in the following blanks.

_____ (program) >>>> _____
(program) >>>> _____ (program) >>>>
_____ (program)

3. Unite All Ministries around the Process (Alignment)

As you begin to implement your discipleship process, pursue alignment early in implementation. If you lead a student ministry and there are no other ministries that you oversee, then be sure all leaders and teams that serve in your ministry understand their role in the process.

If you oversee multiple ministries or campuses, implement the same simple process in each ministry. Using the same language will help students remember the vision and will encourage unity.

Remind leaders of the process often and how their role is vital to the success of the process. When recruiting a volunteer, keep the process at the center of the conversation. The leader's commitment to the process is greater than the abilities he brings to the ministry.

4. Begin to Eliminate (Focus)

You must fight to keep your ministry focused on the process. Focus does not happen naturally; deviation does. Complexity is natural. Simplicity requires constant engagement and leadership.

Removing unnecessary programs will be the toughest aspect of transitioning to a simple student ministry. There will be sentimental and emotional attachment by some leaders and students to programs that are removed. You may even see and hear some wide-eyed, voice-raised type of "reasoning." *Why would you cancel a conference where everybody goes and feels close to God and each other? Why would you cut that? Don't* you *love Jesus anymore?*

You must exercise great caution in removing programs. When you cut a program or event that's important to students, they may feel you're telling them their "needs" aren't important. Pray about the proper timing for removing programs. But once the decision is made, stick with it.

Clear and careful communication will help ease the anxiety around a removed program. If you clearly articulate why the program was removed and how the students will benefit, the transition will make more sense.

Over time you will be able to eliminate everything that doesn't fit within the process. Don't be in a hurry to do this in spite of the tension you feel to push forward. Be prayerful. Be patient. Be humble.

As you discuss and genuinely live out your process, leaders and students will start to see the big picture. Most leaders and students in your ministry will appreciate the focus on intentional discipleship.

As your simple process is consistently discussed and programs and activities are evaluated in light of the process, simple will become part of your ministry DNA.

Simple student ministries implement a process that's clear and moves people through growing stages of discipleship. Every aspect of your ministry must be aligned around the process, and you must fight to stay simple.

Perhaps God has given you a new and fresh vision for student ministry, a new-wine type of vision. A vision free from clutter, free from deviation, and free from complexity.

It's time to craft a new wineskin.

Are you ready? The clock is ticking.

DISCUSSION QUESTIONS

1. Why is change so difficult for people?
2. How different would our ministry look in two years if we implemented a simple process?
3. Do we sense the urgency to change?
4. How can we begin to cultivate a culture of change in our student ministry?
5. How receptive would our students and leaders be to change? Our church?
6. What will be our biggest roadblock to change? How do we deal with it?

About the Authors

Eric Geiger serves as one of the vice presidents at LifeWay Christian Resources, leading the Resources Division. Eric received his doctorate in leadership and church ministry from Southern Seminary. He has authored or coauthored several books including *Creature of the Word* and the bestselling church leadership book, *Simple Church*. Eric is married to Kaye, and they have two daughters.

Jeff Borton is the next generation pastor at Long Hollow Baptist Church in Nashville, Tennessee. He is passionate about discipleship, missions, and seeing students' lives transformed for God's glory. Jeff and his wife, Jen, have three sons. You may contact Jeff at www.jeffborton.blogspot.com.

Notes

Chapter Two

1. Thom S. Rainer and Eric Geiger, *Simple Church* (Nashville, TN: B&H Publishing Group, 2006), 3.

2. Mark Kelly, "LifeWay Research: Parents, Churches Can Help Teens Stay in Church," www.lifeway.com.

Chapter Three

1. Jeff Foxworthy and David Boyd, *You Might Be a Redneck If . . . This Is the Biggest Book You Have Ever Read* (Nashville, TN: Thomas Nelson Publishers, 2004), 272, 9.

2. Metropolitan Transit Authority, "Grand Central," www.grandcentralterminal.com.

3. "Nike and the Swoosh," *Nikebiz*, www.Nike.com.

Chapter Four

1. Bill Breen, "Living in Dell Time," *Fast Company 88* (November 2004), 1.

2. Scarmanga, "Willow Creek Repents?," *Christianity Today*, November 18, 2007, www.christianitytoday.com.

3. Kenneth Boa, *Conformed to His Image: Biblical and Practical Approaches to Spiritual Formation* (Grand Rapids, MI: Zondervan, 2001), 123.

4. Richard Foster, *Celebration of Discipline* (New York, NY: HarperCollins, 1998), 7.

5. Malcom Gladwell, *The Tipping Point* (New York, NY: Little, Brown and Company, 2000), 96–98.

Chapter Five

1. Bruce Jones and David Callahan, "Leadership Talent Emerges During Hurricane Katrina Aviation Rescue Operations." *USCG Leadership News*, Fall 2005, United States Coast Guard.

2. Doug Sample, "Coast Guard School Tough Swimming, Few Pass Rescue Course," American Armed Forces Press Services, www.Defenselink.mil, September 12, 2004.

3. Jerry Useem, "Apple: America's Best Retailer." *Fortune*, March 8, 2007.

Chapter Six

1. International Civil Aviation Organization, "Shooting Down of a Korean Air Lines Boeing 747 (Flight KE 007) on Aug. 31, 1983," August 1993.

2. Chip and Dan Heath, *Made to Stick: Why Some Ideas Survive and Others Die* (New York, NY: Random House, 2007), 29.

3. E-mail from Kyle MacDonald to the author on February 28, 2008.

Chapter Ten

1. E. M. Bounds, *The Complete Works of E.M. Bounds on Prayer* (Grand Rapids, MI: Baker Books, 2004), 390.

2. Jim Collins, *Good to Great: Why Some Companies Make the Leap . . . and Others Don't* (New York, NY: HarperCollins, 2001), 21.